The Word Of The Buddha: An Outline Of The Ethico-Philosophical System Of The Buddha, In The Words Of The Pali Canon

Bhikkhu Nyanatiloka

THE WORD
OF THE BUDDHA.

An outline of the ethico-philosophical
system of the Buddha, in the words of
the Pali Canon, together with Explan-
atory Notes.

By

BHIKKHU NYĀNATILOKA.

TRANSLATED FROM THE GERMAN

By

SASANAVAMSA.

" One thing only, Brothers, do I make known:
Suffering and Deliverance from Suffering."

Rangoon, 1907.
International Buddhist Society.

PREFACE.

I TAKE the liberty of prefacing a few words to the present English edition of " Das Wort des Buddha " which has been prepared from the German edition by the late Superintendent of the Buddhasāsana Samāgama, Mr. J. F. M'Kechnie, now known as Sāsanavaṁsa.

I would wish the Reader to know that " The Word of the Buddha " is not intended as an introduction to the teaching of the Buddha, or as a book on Buddhism merely to be read through and then laid aside. Its aims are, to provide a systematically arranged outline of the Buddha's doctrine for the benefit of such as are already acquainted with its fundamental ideas, and to bring under a single aspect the various parts of that doctrine which at first sight appear to have no connection with one another, but which in fact, when viewed from this aspect, are found all to converge upon a single point,—Deliverance from Suffering,—as expressed by the Buddha Himself in the words I have used as motto :—" One thing only, Brothers, do I make known :— Suffering and Deliverance from Suffering."

Thus it is that the teaching of the Eightfold Path leading to the cessation of suffering constitutes the real essence of Buddhist doctrine, and only from the standpoint of that teaching do the different details find their due place.

I have given these expositions of Buddhist doctrine in the Buddha's own words, having brought them together from the five Nikāyas or Collections of the Sutta-Piṭaka of the Pāli Canon. They have been put together in such a way as to form a connected whole, and thus provide, as it were, a guiding clue to the huge labyrinth of the Sutta-Piṭaka.

The notes, it may be added, are taken from the authoritative Pāli commentaries by Buddhaghosa and from the Abhidhamma. Very rarely have I used my own words. In this English edition they have been considerably expanded, and an Appendix has been added which throws light from another direction, so to speak, upon the Eightfold Path.

Great care has been taken to render the present work an accurate compendium of the teaching of the Buddha ; how far that care has resulted in success, I must leave to the judgment of my Readers.

NYÂNATILOKA.

926

❧ CORRIGENDA. ❧

			for :—	read :—
Note	9,	line 2 from the bottom	will	may.
„	11, last	„ 17	page 40.	„ page 27.
Page 15,		„ 18	) self-affirming Action or Kamma.	„ (self-affirming Action or Kamma.)
„ 15,			Delete :—ceases ; with the cessation of self-affirming Action.	
Note 15,		„ 4 and 5	„ Wrong Attentiveness, & Wrong Concentration.	
Page 27,		„ 10		read in the margin :— Dependent Origination.
			for :—page 100	read :—pages 19 and 20.
„ 27,		„ 11	„ Note 9	„ Note 10.
„ 28,		„ 13	„ Note 9	„ Note 13.
„ 28, last				
Note 49,		„ 3	„ every evil thought	„ many evil thoughts.
„ 50,		„ 8	„ Note 22	„ Note 23.
„ 50,		„ 15	„ Note 9	„ Note 13.

CONTENTS.

THE WORD
OF THE BUDDHA.

Namo Tassa Bhagavato Arahato,
Sammāsambuddhassa !

The Word of the Buddha [1]

OR

THE FOUR HOLY TRUTHS.

THE Perfect One (Tathāgata) [2] Brothers, the Holy One, the Fully Enlightened One (Buddha), at Isipatana, in the deer-park at Benares, has established the supreme kingdom of Truth, and none can withstand it,—neither ascetic nor priest, nor invisible being, nor good nor evil spirit, nor anyone whatsoever in all the world ; it is the making known, the pointing out, the laying down, the setting forth, the unveiling, the explaining, the making evident, of the Four Holy Truths.

1. The " Buddha," The Enlightened One, is the title of honour bestowed upon the Indian sage, Gotama, the founder of that ethico-philosophical system known to Europe by the name of Buddhism. He was born about the year six hundred before Christ, as the son of one of the princes of Northern India, not far from the borders of modern Nepal. Up to his twenty-ninth year—the year in which he renounced the world and exchanged his princely life for that of a homeless mendicant—he lived with his wife. the Princess Yasodhara, who bore him a son named Rāhula, the same who later became one of his favourite disciples.

The teaching of the Buddha, the " Dhamma" (Law, Truth) is set forth in the three collections of the sacred writings, the Tipiṭaka (literally, three baskets), named respectively The Vinaya Piṭaka, The Sutta Piṭaka, and The Abhidhamma Piṭaka. The Vinaya Piṭaka for the most part, contains the mere regulations that govern the life of the monk ; the Doctrine of Deliverance, again, as set forth in the " Four Holy Truths", is treated of in the Sutta Piṭaka or " Collection of Discourses" ; whilst the Abhidhamma Piṭaka is exclusively concerned with profound psychological enquiries.

The " Sangha " (literally, Assemblage) is the order of Mendicant Monks (Bhikkhus) founded by the Buddha, and is the oldest order of mendicants in the world. Its most famous members in the Buddha's day were : Sāriputta, who, after the Master himself, possessed the profoundest knowledge of the Doctrine ;—Moggallāna, who had the greatest super-human powers ;—Ananda, the favourite disciple and constant companion of the Buddha ;—Kassapa, the president of the council held at Rajagaha immediately after the Buddha's death ;—Anuruddha the metaphysician, and Rāhula the Buddha's own son. The Judas among the disciples was Devadatta, the Buddha's nephew.

At the present day the total number of those who hold the Buddha in reverence, in Burma, Siam, Ceylon, India, Japan, China, Tibet and elsewhere amounts to about five hundred millions, that is to say,—to about one-third of the human race. The threefold confession of these runs as follows :—

Buddhaṁ saranaṁ gacchāmi.
Dhammaṁ saranaṁ gacchāmi.
Saṅghaṁ saranaṁ gacchāmi.

Expressed in English :—

I put my trust in the Buddha.
I put my trust in the Truth.
I put my trust in the Holy Brotherhood.

2. A title of Gotama Buddha. The following titles are also used: Bhagavā, the Blessed One ; Sakyamuni, the Sage of the Tribe of the Sakyas ; Sugata, the Welcome One, and many others.

What are these Four Holy Truths? The Holy Truth of Suffering, the Holy Truth of the Cause of Suffering, the Holy Truth of the Cessation of Suffering, the Holy Truth of the Path that leads to the Cessation of Suffering.

And the Blessed One said: So long, Brothers, as my knowledge and insight as regards each one of these Four Holy Truths was not quite clear, so long was I doubtful as to whether I had won to complete insight into that knowledge which is unsurpassed in the heavens and upon the earth, unexcelled among all the hosts of ascetics and priests, of invisible beings and of men. But so soon, Brothers, as my knowledge and insight as regards each one of these Four Holy Truths had become perfectly clear, there arose in me the assurance that I had won to complete comprehension of that knowledge which is unsurpassed in the heavens and upon the earth, unexcelled among all the hosts of ascetics and priests, of invisible beings and of men.

And that deep knowledge have I made my own,—that knowledge, difficult to perceive, difficult to understand, peace-bestowing, and which cannot be gained by mere reasoning; which is profound and only accessible to the wise disciple.

The world however is given to pleasure, ensnared in pleasure, enchanted with pleasure. Verily those that are given to pleasure, ensnared in pleasure, enchanted with pleasure will hardly understand the Law of Causation, the conditionality of *Dependent Origination* (Paṭiccasamuppāda); incomprehensible also will be to them the cessation of all existence, the freeing one's self from every form of Becoming, the Annihilation of Craving (taṇhā), the turning away from Desire ; cessation and Nibbāna.

Yet among beings there are some whose eyes are only a little darkened with dust : they will perceive the Truth (Dhamma).

THE FIRST TRUTH.

THE HOLY TRUTH OF SUFFERING.

The purport of the First Truth. What now Brothers, is the Holy Truth of Suffering?

Birth is Suffering; decay is Suffering; disease is Suffering; Death is Suffering; Sorrow, Lamentation, Pain, Grief and Despair are Suffering; not to get what one desires, is Suffering; in short, the Five Aspects of Existence are Suffering.

What now, Brothers, is Birth? The birth, the bearing, the germination, the conception, the manifestation of the Aspects of Existence of Beings belonging to this or that order of Beings; the arising of sense-activity;—this, Brothers, is called Birth.[3]

What now, Brothers, is Decay? The becoming aged and withered, decrepit, grey and wrinkled of beings belonging to this or the other order of beings; the disappearance of the vital force, the enfeebling of the senses;—this, Brothers, is called Decay.

What now, Brothers, is Death? The parting, the disappearance, of Beings out of this or that Order of Beings; the rending asunder, the ruin, the death, the dissolution, the end of the life-period, the disappearance of the Aspects of Existence, the putrefaction of the corpse;—this, Brothers, is called Death.

What now, Brothers, is Sorrow? What soever, Brothers, through this or the other loss which one undergoes, through this or the other misfortune which one encounters— is sorrow, trouble, affliction, inward distress, inward woe,— this, Brothers, is called Sorrow.

What now, Brothers, is Lamentation? Whatsoever, Brothers, through this or the other loss which one undergoes, through this or the other misfortune which one encounters—is plaint and lamentation, wailing and bemoaning, mourning and unalloyed lamentation;—this, Brothers; is called Lamentation.

---

3. By birth (Jāti) is to be understood the entire birth-process, beginning with conception and ending with parturition.

What now, Brothers, is Pain? Whatsoever, Brothers, is painful to the body, disagreeable to the body; is felt by bodily contact to be painful and disagreeable;—this, Brothers, is called Pain.

What now, Brothers, is Grief? Whatsoever, Brothers is painful to the mind, disagreeable to the mind; is felt by mental contact to be painful and disagreeable;—this, Brothers, is called Grief.

What now, Brothers, is Despair? Whatsoever, Brothers, through this or the other loss which one undergoes, through this or the other sorrow which one encounters,—is dejection and despairing, despondency and hopelessness;—this, Brothers, is called Despair.

What now, Brothers, is the Suffering of not getting what one desires? To beings, Brothers, subject to birth, comes the desire: "O that we were not subject to birth! O that no birth (again) lay before us!" But that cannot be got by mere desiring and not to get what one desires is Suffering. To beings, Brothers, subject to decay, disease, death, sorrow, lamentation, pain, grief and despair, comes the desire: "O that we were not subject to decay, disease, death, sorrow, lamentation, pain, grief and despair! O that there lay before us nor decay, nor disease, nor death; neither sorrow, nor lamentation, nor pain, neither grief nor despair!" But this cannot be got by mere desiring; and not to get what one desires is Suffering.

What now, in brief, Brothers, are the Five Aspects (Khandhas) of Existence? They are, Material Existence (Rūpa), Sensation (Vedanā), Perception (Saññā), Subjective Differentiations (Saṅkhārā, mental properties), Consciousness (Viññāṇa).

The five Khandhas or Aspects of Existence.

All material existence, Brothers, whether one's own or not one's own, whether gross or refined, lofty or low, far or near,—this belongs to the Aspect of Material Existence (rūpa-kkhandha); all sensation belongs to the Aspect of Sensation; all perception belongs to the Aspect of Perception; all differentiations belong to the Aspect of Subjective

Differentiations ; all consciousness belongs to the Aspect of Consciousness.[4]

Rupa-kkhandha or the Material Aspect. What now, Brothers, is the Aspect of Material Existence ? It is the Four Chief Material Elements and the bodily properties dependent upon the Four Chief Material Elements.

The four Elements (elementary forces.) What now, Brothers, are the Four Chief Material Elements ? They are the Solid Element (Pathavī-dhātu), the Fluid Element (Apodhātu), the Heating Element (Tejo-dhātu), the Vibrating Element (Vāyo-dhātu).[5]

1. What now, Brothers, is the *Solid Element* (Pathavī-dhātu) ? There is the Solid Element of one's own body and the Solid Element of other bodies. What now, Brothers, is the Solid Element of one's own body ? Whatsoever, of one's own body individualised, presents itself hard and solid as the hair of the head, and the body, as the nails, teeth, skin, flesh, sinews, bones, marrow, kidneys, heart, liver, diaphragm, spleen, lungs, stomach, bowels, mesentery, excrement, and whatsoever else of one's own body individualised, presents itself hard and solid—this, Brothers, is called the Solid Element of one's own body. Whatever there is of the Solid Element in one's own body, and whatever there is of the Solid Element in other bodies, this is the Solid Element ; hence one should understand according to reality and true

---

4. Our individual existence is nothing more than the subjective-objective *Anschauung*, Nāma-Rūpa, produced by consciousness, the existence of which latter again is conditioned by the contact of the six senses—the mind being the sixth—with their corresponding objects. Material Existence constitutes the objective aspect (Rūpa-kkhandha), whilst the subjective aspects (Nāma-kkhandhas) consist of Sensation, Perception, Subjective Differentiations, and Consciousness. We shall see later on that these five Khandhas or Aspects of Existence, whether taken collectively or apart, do not constitute any kind of self-existent state or *Ding an Sich*, or anything that can be called an ' I', in the absolute sense of the word, and that hence the belief in the existence of such an ' I' is a purely illusory belief.

5. The Four Elements, or—to speak more correctly—the Four Elementary Forces, Pathavī-dhātu, Apo-dhātu, Tejo-dhātu, and Vāyo-dhātu may be rendered as, Inertia, Cohesion, (bandhana-lakkhana), Radiation, and Vibration (calana-lakkhana).

All material things, according to Buddhism owe their existence to the more or less dissimilar inter-blending of these forces. The twenty-four bodily properties which depend upon these forces are :—1. Eye 2. Ear 3. Nose. 4. Tongue. 5. Body. 6. Form. 7. Sound. 8. Odour. 9. Taste 10. Masculinity. 11. Feminity. 12. Vitality. 13. Heart. (European science would here say, *brain*, since by *heart* is meant the organ of thinking.) 14. Gesture. 15. Speech. 16. Space. (*i. e.*, cavities, as of the ear, the nose, and so forth.) 17. Agility. 18. Elasticity, 19. Adaptability. 20. Growth. 21. Duration. 22. Decay. 23. Variability. 24. Change of substance.

(For a detailed description of the foregoing, consult the Visuddhi-Magga.)

wisdom : This does not belong to me ; this am I not ; this is no " I " (Attā).[6]

2. What now, Brothers, is the *Fluid Element* (Apo-dhātu) ? There is the Fluid Element of one's own body and the Fluid Element of other bodies. What now, Brothers, is the Fluid Element of one's own body ? Whatever, indivi-dualised presents itself fluid and watery, in one's own body, as bile, phlegm, pus, blood, sweat, lymph, tears, serum, spit-tle, nasal mucus, oil of the joints, urine, and whatever else individualised presents itself fluid and watery in one's own body—this Brothers, is called the fluid Element in one's own body. Whatever there is of the Fluid Element in one's own body, and whatever there is of the Fluid Element in other bodies,—this is the Fluid Element ; hence one should under-stand according to reality and true wisdom : This does not belong to me ; this am I not ; this is no ' I.'

3. What now, Brothers, is the *Heating Element* (Tejo-dhātu)? There is the Heating Element of one's own body and the Heating Element of other bodies. What now, Bro-thers, is the Heating Element of one's own body ? Whatso-ever, individualised, presents itself fiery and flame-like in one's own body as that whereby heat and the process of combustion arise, whereby one grows hot, whereby that which one has eaten, drunken, or masticated or tasted, is di-gested ; or whatever else individualised, presents itself fiery and flame-like in one's own body,—this, Brothers, is called the Heating Element in one's own body. Whatever now there is of the Heating Element in one's own body and what-ever there is of the Heating Element in other bodies,—this is the Heating Element ; hence one should understand accord-ing to reality and true wisdom : This does not belong to me ; this am I not ; this is no ' I.'

4. What now, Brothers, is the *Vibrating Element* (Vayo-dhātu) ? There is the Vibrating Element of one's own

---

6. Just as the word chariot is merely a designation for axle, wheels body, shaft, and other parts put together in a certain manner,—and as, when we proceed to investigate this particular thing we discover that in the abso-lute sense there is no chariot there ;—and just as the word *house* is nothing more than a convenient designation for wood and other materials, which put together, after a specific fashion, constitute an enclosed space, and yet in the absolute sense there is no house at all there ;—in exactly the same way that which we call a being or an individual is nothing more than the presence of the Five Khandhas or Aspects of Existence, and when we proceed to in-quire into the Khandhas,—each one separately by itself,—we come to the knowledge that in the absolute sense there is nothing present that can fur-nish any real support for such fictions as : ' I am,' or ' I.'

(*Visuddhi Magga.*)

body and the Vibrating Element of other bodies. What now, Brothers, is the Vibrating Element of one's own body ? Whatsoever, individualised, presents itself mobile and fugitive in one's own body, as the upward-going and the downward-going vapours, the vapours of stomach and intestines, the in-breathing and the out-breathing ; or whatsoever else individualised, presents itself mobile and fugitive in one's own body—this, Brothers, is called the Vibrating Element in one's own body. Whatsoever there is of the Vibrating Element in one's own body and whatsoever there is of the Vibrating Element in other bodies,—this is the Vibrating Element ; hence one should understand according to reality and true wisdom : This does not belong to me ; this am I not ; this is no ' I '.

Just as Brothers, one calls a house the circumscribed space, which comes to be by means of beams and rushes, reeds and clay ;—even so Brothers, we call body, the circumscribed space that arises by means of bones and sinews, flesh and skin.

If now Brothers, one's eye is whole, and external forms do not fall upon the field of vision, and no corresponding conjunction takes place, then there occurs no formation of the corresponding consciousness-impression. If one's eye is whole and external forms do fall upon the field of vision, and still no corresponding conjunction takes place, then also there occurs no formation of a corresponding consciousness-impression.

If however, Brothers, one's eye is whole, and external forms fall upon the field of vision and a corresponding conjunction takes place, in that case there occurs the formation of the corresponding consciousness-impressions.

Hence I say : The arising of consciousness is dependent upon causes, and without these there is no consciousness. Now upon whatsoever causes the arising of consciousness is dependent, after these causes it is called.

Consciousness whose arising depends on the eye (Cakkhu) and forms, is called eye-consciousness (Cakkhuviññāṇa.)

Consciousness whose arising depends on the ear (Sota) and sounds, is called ear-consciousness (Sotaviññāṇa).

Consciousness whose arising depends on the nose (Ghāna) and odours, is called olfactory-consciousness (Ghānaviññāṇa).

Consciousness whose arising depends on the tongue
(Jivhā) and tastes, is called tongue-consciousness (Jivhāviñ-
ñāna.)

Consciousness whose arising depends on the body
(Kāya) and bodily-contacts, is called body-consciousness
(Kāyaviññāna.)

Consciousness whose arising depends on the mind
(Mano) and ideas, is called thought-consciousness (Mano-
vinnāna.)[8]

Whatsoever there is of material existence in the consciousness that arises in each instance,—that belongs to the
Aspect of Material Existence. Whatsoever there is of sensation therein,—that belongs to the Aspect of Sensation.
Whatsoever there is of perception therein,—that belongs to
the Aspect of Perception. Whatsoever there are of differentiations therein,—that belongs to the Aspect of Subjective
Differentiations (mental properties). Whatsoever there is of
consciousness therein,—that belongs to the Aspect of Con-
ciousness. And it is impossible, Brothers, that any one can
explain the passing out of the existence and the entering
into a new existence, or the growth, increase and development of consciousness, independent of Material Existence,
independent of Sensation, independent of Perception, independent of the Subjective Differentiations.

All things, Brothers, are transient. The body is tran-
The three Cha- sient, Sensation is transient, Perception is
racteristics of transient, the Subjective Differentiations are
existence. transient, Consciousness is transient.

But that which is transient,—that is suffering ; and
whatsoever is transient, painful and subject to change,—of
that one cannot rightly say : "This belongs to me ; this
am I ; this is my ' I '."

Wherefore, Brothers, whatever there be of Material Existence, whatever there be of Sensation, of Perception, of
Subjective Differentiations, or of Consciousness, whether
one's own or another's, whether gross or refined, lofty or
low, far or near, one should understand according to
reality and true wisdom : " This does not belong to me ;
this am I not ; this is no ' I ' (Attā)."

---

7. The objects of vision are not bodies—these latter can only be known
through the sense of bodily touch—they are forms, existing,—so to speak—
like pictures in one plane, the figures in which are dependent upon differences
of colour and of lighting.

8. Thought-consciousness, or, inward consciousness is, as it were, a
mirror in which all external consciousness-impressions,—forms, sounds, etc.,
—are reflected.

Whoso Brothers, delights in the body, delights in Sensation, delights in Perception, delights in the Differentiations, delights in Consciousness,—he delights in suffering, and whoso delights in suffering, shall not obtain release from suffering. Thus I say.

How can you laugh, how take delight in earthly things? Verily you walk in darkness! Did you never

The Three Warnings. yet see among you a man or a woman, eighty, ninety, or an hundred years old? decrepit, crooked as a gable-roof, bowed forward, supported on a staff, staggering along with tottering steps, wretched, youth long since fled, toothless, bleached hair hanging in wisps over the blotched and wrinkled brow? And did the thought never come to you then: "I also am subject to Decay; by no means can I escape it"?

Did you never see amongst you men or women who, laden with grievous disease, twisted with pain, wallowed in their own filth, and when they had been lifted up, were obliged to lie down again? And did the thought never come to you then: "I also am subject to Disease; by no means can I escape it"?

Did you never see amongst you a corpse that had lain for one, two, or three days, swollen up, blue-black in colour, a prey to corruption? And did the thought never come to you then: "I also am subject to Death; by no means can I escape it"?

Without beginning or end, Brothers, is this Saṁsāra.[9]

Samsara. Unperceivable is the beginning of Beings buried in blindness, who, seized of craving, are ever and again brought to new birth and so hasten, through the endless round of re-births.

What think you, Brothers? Which is greater,—the floods of tears which, weeping and wailing you have shed upon this long way, ever and again hastening towards new

---

9. Saṁsāra (literally, wandering) is the name by which is designated the sea of life ever restlessly heaving up and down, the symbol of the process of ever again and again being born, growing old, suffering, and dying. More precisely put: Saṁsāra is the unbroken chain of the groups of the Five Aspects of Existence or Khandhas which, constantly changing from moment to moment, follow continuously one upon the other through inconceivable periods of time. Of this Saṁsāra, a single life time constitutes only a vanishingly tiny fraction; hence, to be able to comprehend the First Holy Truth, one must let his gaze rest upon Saṁsāra, upon the apparently endless chain of re-births, and not merely upon an insignificantly small particle of the same; for this latter, as being only a single phenomenon will of course seem the less painful.

birth and new death, united to the undesired, separated from the desired,—this, or the waters of the Four Great Seas ?

Long time, Brothers, have you suffered the death of a mother, for long the death of a father, for long the death of a son, for long the death of a daughter, for long the death of brothers and sisters; long time have ye undergone the loss of your goods, long time have you been afflicted with disease. And because you have experienced the death of a mother, the death of a father, the death of a son, the death of a daughter, the death of brothers and sisters, the loss of goods, the pangs of disease, having been united with the un-desired and separated from the desired, you have verily shed more tears upon this long way,—hastening from birth to death, from death to birth—than all the waters that are held in the Four Great Seas.

What think you, Brothers ? Which is greater,—the blood that through your execution, has flowed upon this long way, whilst you have hastened ever and again to new birth and new death,—this, or the waters of the Four Great Seas ?

Long time, Brothers, condemned as murderers, have you by your execution, verily shed more blood than all the waters that are held in the Four Great Seas. Long time Brothers, arrested as robbers, have you by your execution verily shed more blood than all the waters that are held in the Four Great Seas. Long time, Brothers, caught in adultery have you through your execution verily shed more blood than all the waters that are held in the Four Great Seas.

But how is this possible? Without beginning or end, Brothers, is this Saṁsāra; Unperceivable is the beginning of Beings buried in blindness, who, seized of craving, are ever and again brought to new birth and so hasten through the endless round of re-births.

And thus, Brothers, have you long time undergone suf-fering, undergone torment, undergone misfortune and filled the graveyards full,—verily, Brothers, long enough to be dissatisfied with all existence,—long enough to turn your-selves away from all suffering,—long enough to release yourselves from it all.

SECOND TRUTH.

THE HOLY TRUTH OF THE CAUSE OF SUFFERING.

The threefold Craving. What now, Brothers, is the Holy Truth of the Cause of Suffering? It is that Craving (Taṇhā)[10] which gives rise to fresh re-birth, and bound by greed for pleasure, now here, now there, finds ever fresh delight. It is the Sensual Craving (Kāma-taṇhā), the Craving for Individual Existence (Bhava-taṇhā), the Craving for temporal happiness (Vibhava-taṇhā.)[11]

---

10. It is no real being, no self-determined, unchangeable ' I ' that is re-born. Moreover there is no being that remains the same even for two conse-cutive moments, for the five Khandhas or Aspects of Existence are in a state of perpetual change, of continual dissolution and renewal. As one thing they disappear, and re-appear the next moment as something wholly new. Hence it follows that there is no such thing as a real being (esse)—there is only an endless process of change, of becoming; and this becoming, in its inner essence is Action (Kamma), caused and causing, individualised and individu-alising.

Just as the wave that apparently hastens over the surface of a pond, is nothing more than a manifested effect of the continuous rising and falling of that surface, produced by the wind :—in exactly the same way there is no real *I*-unit, that hastens through the sea of repeated births, but only an effect (Kamma) caused by Taṇhā (The Impulse to Life) which, according to the character of its working (Cf. The Knowledge of Good and Evil, page 28,) manifests itself here as a man and there as an animal or as some invisible being, which again with their perpetually repeated being born and decaying again, may be compared with the perpetually repeated rising and falling of the water.

It follows that existence (Becoming) or,—otherwise expressed--Action or Kamma, does not as it were *belong* to the man, but *is* the man himself; and the man—as also after its own fashion, the wave—is at every moment the exact result of all past bodily, verbal, and mental action or Kamma, and at the same time the cause of all future action. As it is said in the Aṅguttara Nikāya :—" My deed is my possession. My deed is mine inheritance. My deed is the mother's womb that bears me. My deed is the tribe from which I spring. My deed is my refuge."

11. Bhava-taṇhā is the Craving for individual existence and is in-timately connected with spiritualistic beliefs in an absolute *I*-essence or 'soul' persisting independently even after the death of the material body. (Sassata-diṭṭhi, Belief in Eternity.)

Vibhava-taṇhā is the Craving to so order this present brief existence that it may yield as much enjoyment as possible. This craving is the direct out-come of the delusive materialistic notion of a more or less real *I*-hood, ex-isting during our lifetime but not standing in any kind of causal connection with the time before birth and the time after death ; hence, a mere toy, ex-isting through the pure caprice of nature. It will be clear to everyone that such a delusive idea, once it really takes possession of a man's thoughts and feelings and is carried to its logical conclusion, must of necessity lead either to the deepest abysses of moral depravity, or to a profound life-despair and the consequent anathematisation of those to whom one owes one's entry into life. (Cf. Note 24 and the Two Extremes and the Middle Doctrine, page 40.)

But where, Brothers, does this Craving take its rise and where does it spring up ? Where does it find a foothold and where does it strike its roots ?

The six Sense-domains. The eye is delightful, is pleasureable to men ; there this craving takes its rise, there it flourishes, there finds a foothold, there strikes its roots. Ear, nose, tongue, body, and mind (mano) are delightful, are pleasureable to men : there this craving takes its rise, there it springs up, there finds a foothold, there strikes its roots.

The six Sense-objects. Forms, sounds, odours, tastes, bodily contacts and ideas (objects of the mind) are delightful, are pleasureable to men; there this craving takes its rise, there it springs up, there finds a foothold, there strikes its roots.

The six-fold Consciousness. The consciousness that arises through the contact of eye, ear, nose, tongue, body, and mind [with their appropriate objects] is delightful, is pleasureable to men ; there this craving takes its rise, there it springs up, there finds a foothold, there strikes its roots.

The six-fold Contact. The contact that arises through eye, ear, nose, tongue body, and mind, is delightful, is pleasureable to men ; there this craving takes its rise, there it springs up, there finds a foothold, there strikes its roots.

The six-fold Sensation. The sensations that arise through seeing, hearing, smelling, tasting, touching, and thinking, are delightful, are pleasureable to men there this craving takes its rise, there it springs up, there finds a foothold, there strikes its roots.

The six-fold Perception and Ideation. Perception and ideation of forms, sounds, odours, tastes, bodily contacts, ideas, are delightful, are pleasureable to men ; there this craving takes its rise, there it springs up, there finds a foothold, there strikes its roots.

The six-fold Craving. The craving for forms, for sounds, for odours, for tastes, for bodily contact, and for ideas, is delightful, is pleasureable to men ; there this craving takes its rise, there it springs up, there finds a foothold, there strikes its roots.

Thinking and reflecting over forms, over sounds, over odours, over tastes, over bodily contacts **The six-fold Thinking and Reflecting.** and over ideas, is delightful, is pleasureable to men; there this craving takes its rise, there it springs up, there finds a foothold, there strikes its roots.

Thus, Brothers, one beholds a form,[12] with the eye, hears a sound with the ear, smells an odour with the nose, experiences a taste with the tongue, feels a contact with the body, cognises an idea with the mind. If now the form, sound, odour, taste, bodily contact or idea, is pleasureable, one is seized with longing therefore, and if unpleasant, with aversion.

Now whatever sort of sensation (Vedanā) he experiences, **The Origin of Becoming.** a pleasant sensation or an unpleasant sensation or a neutral sensation, he approves of and cherishes the sensation and clings to it, and whilst he approves of and cherishes the sensation and clings to it, desire springs up in him; but desire after sensations means Clinging to Existence (upādāna); Clinging to Existence causes the Process of Becoming (Bhava); the process of Becoming (self-affirming action or Kamma) produces future Birth (jāti); Birth gives rise to decay and death, sorrow, lamentation, pain, grief and despair. Thus arises the whole mass of suffering.

This, Brothers, is called the Holy Truth of the Cause of Suffering.

Impelled verily by sensuous Craving attracted by sensuous Craving, moved by sensuous Craving, **The visible Cause of Suffering.** only out of vain Craving, kings war with kings, princes with princes, priests with priests, citizens with citizens; the mother quarrels with the son, the son with the mother, the father with the son, the son with the father; brother quarrels with brother, brother with sister, sister with brother, friend with friend. Thus given to dissension, quarrelling and fighting, they fall upon one another with stones, sticks, and swords. And so they hasten towards death, or deathly hurt. But this, Brothers, is the misery of sensuous craving, is the visible Cause of Suffering, arisen through sensuous Craving, brought about through sensuous Craving, upheld by sensuous Craving, absolutely dependent upon sensuous Craving.

---

12. Strictly speaking, it is the eye-consciousness that perceives forms by means of the sensitivity of the eye; hence the eye of itself cannot see but is merely a means of seeing. The like holds good of ear, nose, tongue, and body.

And further, Brothers, attracted by sensuous Craving, moved by sensuous Craving, only out of vain Craving, people break contracts, rob others of their possessions, steal, betray, seduce married women. Then kings have such criminals caught and condemn them to be beaten with whips, sticks, or rods; to have their hands, or their feet, or both hands and feet cut off; to be torn in pieces by dogs, to be impaled alive, to be beheaded. And so they hasten towards death or deathly hurt. But this, Brothers, is the misery of sensuous Craving, is the visible Cause of Suffering arisen through sensuous Craving, brought about through sensuous Craving, upheld by sensuous Craving, absolutely dependent upon sensuous Craviug.

And further, Brothers, impelled by sensuous Craving attracted by sensuous Craving, only out of **The concealed Cause of Suffering.** vain Craving, they walk the evil way in deeds, the evil way in words, the evil way in thoughts; and walking the evil way in deeds, the evil way in words, the evil way in thoughts, at the dissolution of the body, after death they go downwards to a state of suffering, they come to ruin and disaster, for it is said : "Nor in the air, nor in the ocean's depths, nor in the mountain caves nor anywhere in all the worlds, find'st thou a place where thou art freed from evil deeds." (Cf. Note 10.) But this, Brothers, is the misery of sensuous Craving, is the concealed Cause of suffering arisen through sensuous Craving, brought about through sensuous Craving, upheld by sensuous Craving, absolutely dependent upon sensuous craving.

There will come a time, Brothers, when the great world-ocean will dry up, vanish and be no more. But verily, Brothers, there is no end to the Suffering of beings buried in blindness, who, seized by craving are ever brought again and again to renewed birth and hasten through the endless round of rebirths.

There will come a time, Brothers, when the mighty earth will be devoured by fire, perish and be no more. But, Brothers, verily there is no end to the Suffering of beings buried in blindness, who, seized by Craving are ever brought again and again to renewed birth and hasten through the endless rouud of re-births.

THIRD TRUTH.

THE HOLY TRUTH OF THE CESSATION OF SUFFERING.

What now, Brothers, is the Holy Truth of the Cessation of Suffering?

It is the complete extinction of this Craving, the rejection, dispelling, freeing, getting rid of it.

But how, Brothers, does this Craving come to disappear? Where is it dissolved? Wherever in the world there is the delightful and the pleasureable, there this Craving comes to disappear; there it is dissolved.

The Cessation of the process of Becoming. Thus, Brothers, released from Sensual Craving, (Kāmataṇhā), released from the Craving for Existence (Bhava-taṇhā), one does not return, one does not enter again into the Process of Becoming for, it is even through the total extinction of this Craving, that the Clinging to Existence (Upādānaṁ) ceases; with the cessation of the Clinging to Existence, the Process of Becoming ceases; with the cessation of the Process of Becoming,) self-affirming Action or Kamma ceases; with the cessation of self-affirming Action, Rebirth is done away; through not being reborn, decay, death, sorrow, lamentation, suffering, grief and despair cease. Thus comes about the cessation of the whole mass of suffering.

This, Brothers, is called the holy truth of the Cessation of Suffering.

Nibbana. But this is the Peace, this is the Highest, namely the cessation of all existence, the freeing one's self from every form of Becoming, the annihilation of Craving, the turning away from desire, cessation and Nibbāna; for, excited by Greed (Lobha), Brothers, furious with Anger (Dosa), blinded by Delusion, (Moha), with mind over whelmed, with mind enslaved, men reflect upon their own misfortune, men reflect upon the misfortune of others, men reflect upon the misfortune of both themselves and others, men experience mental suffering and anguish. If however Greed and Anger and Delusion are done away, men reflect neither upon their own misfortune, nor upon the misfortune of others, nor upon the misfortune of both themselves and others, men experience no mental suffering and anguish. Thus, Brothers, is Nibbāna visible in this life and not merely in the future; inviting, attractive, accessible to the wise disciple.

The Araham. And the Saint (Araham) whose peace is no more disturbed by anything whatsoever in all the world, the pure one, the sorrowless, the freed from

Craving (Taṇhā), he has swum across the Ocean of Birth and Decay.

He truly penetrates to the cause of sensations, enlightened is his mind. And for a disciple so delivered, in whose heart dwells peace, there is no longer any pondering over what has been done, and naught more remains for him to do. Just as a rock of one solid mass remains unshaken by the wind, even so, neither forms, nor sounds, nor odours, nor tastes, nor contacts of any kind ; neither the desired nor the undesired can cause such an one to waver. Steadfast is his mind, gained is Deliverance.

Verily, Brothers, there is a condition, where there is **The Unchangeable.** neither the Solid (Paṭhavi), nor the Fluid (Apo) neither Heat (Tejo), nor Motion (Vāyo), neither this world nor any other world, neither sun nor moon.

This, Brothers, I call neither arising nor passing away, neither standing still nor being born nor dying. There, is neither substance nor development nor any basis. This is the End of Suffering.

There is, Brothers, an unborn, an unoriginated, that has not become, that has not been formed. If, Brothers, there were not this unborn, this unoriginated, that has not become, that has not been formed, escape from the world of the born the originated, the become, the formed, would not be possible.

But since, Brothers, there is an unborn, an unoriginated, that has not become, that has not been formed, therefore is escape possible from the world of the born, the originated, the become, the formed.[13]

---

13. Just as the effects produced by the wind, in its manifestations as the rising and falling of the water, give rise to the illusion of a wave apparently hastening over the surface of a pond, and these effects, together with the illusion dependent upon them, come to an end soon after the wind has ceased, —in exactly the same way, the effects (Kamma) produced by Taṇhā (giving rise to the illusion of an *I*-being apparently hastening from birth to birth, through its manifestations, the arising and decaying of the Khandhas) must, when once Taṇhā is extinguished, themselves also shortly thereafter, become wholly extinguished, together with the illusion dependent upon them, namely, the so-called *I*. No annihilation of a personal being has taken place, no cessation of an absolute existence, for that which we call existence is, as we saw, only a continuous arising and passing away, hence, a pure unreality, an illusion ; and the reality, that which knows neither arising nor passing away, neither birth nor death,—which is eternally unchangeable ;—this is precisely the cessation, the extinction (Nibbāna) ot this illusion.

There is thus an extinction (Nibbāna) of Taṇhā (Kilesaparinibbāna, literally, extinction of passion), which takes place even during the lifetime of the Arahaṁ, namely at the moment of his attaining Arahatship, and an extinction of Kamma and of the Khandhas (Khandhaparinibbāna), which takes place at his death.

THE FOURTH TRUTH.

THE HOLY TRUTH OF THE PATH THAT LEADS TO THE CESSATION OF SUFFERING.

The Two Extremes, (Sensuality, Self-mortification) and the Middle Path. To abandon one's self to *Sensuality*, to the base, the common, the vulgar, the unholy, the harmful, and also to abandon one's self to *Self-mortification*, to the painful, the unholy, the harmful:—both these two extremes the Perfect One has rejected, and found out the Middle Path which makes one both to see and to know, which leads to peace, to discernment, to enlightenment and to extinction (Nibbāna).

The Eight-fold Path. It is the "Eight-fold Path," the way that leads to the cessation of suffering, namely:

(1.) Right Understanding Sammādiṭṭhi.[14]	} I.	Paññā, Enlightenment.
(2.) Right Mindedness. Sammāsankappo.		
(3.) Right Speech Sammāvācā.		
(4.) Right Action, Sammākammanto.	} II.	Sīla, Morality.
(5.) Right Living, Sammā-ājivo.		
(6.) Right Effort, Sammāvāyāmo.		
(7.) Right Attentiveness, Sammāsati.	} III.	Samādhi, Concentration.
(8.) Right Concentration, Sammāsamādhi.[15]		

14. All unselfish and higher endeavour is of necessity based upon a certain degree of Right Understanding, whether this endeavour is met with among Buddhists, Hindus, Christians, Muhamedans, or even amongst so-called Materialists; this, in fact, is the very reason why Right Understanding takes rank as the First Link of the Eight-fold Path. The order, however, in which the different links of the Path are brought to perfection is, Sīla, Samādhi, and Paññā, or, in English: Morality, Concentration, and Enlightenment. Right Understanding or Enlightenment is thus the Alpha and the Omega of the entire teaching of the Buddha.

15. In every good thought (Kusala-citta) there are always present at least four Links of the Path, namely, Right Mindedness, Right Effort, Right Attentiveness, Right Concentration. In the same way, every evil thought (Akusala-citta) is accompanied by Wrong Mindedness, Wrong Effort, Wrong Attentiveness, and Wrong Concentration.

2

This, Brothers, is the Middle Path which the Perfect One has found out, which makes one both to see and to know ; which leads to peace, to discernment, to enlightenment, and to extinction which is free from suffering, free from torment, free from lamentation, free from pain, leading right onwards ; and like this way there is no other way.

If you follow this way, you shall find an end of suffer-ing. Yet seek not for any outward help, for each has to struggle for himself; the Perfect Ones (Tathāgatas) only point out the way.

Give ear, Brothers, for the Immortal is found. I reveal, I set forth the Truth. As I reveal it to you, so act and you shall in no long time see face to face, realise, and win, even in this life, to the goal of supreme holiness—that goal[16] for the sake of which sons of good families forsake their homes for the homeless life, and manifest, realise, and ob-tain the perfection of holiness even in this life.

---

16. The goal is Nibbāna.

THE FIRST LINK OF THE PATH.

RIGHT UNDERSTANDING, SAMMA-DITTHI.

What now, Brothers, is Right Understanding?

Understanding of Good and Evil. When, Brothers, the disciple understands Evil and understands the Root of Evil; when he understands Good and understands the Root of Good; this Brothers, is Right Understanding.

What now, Brothers, is Evil (Akusala)?[17]

(1.) Killing, Brothers, is evil.[18] (2.) Stealing is evil. (3.) Unlawful sexual intercourse is evil.	I. Bodily (Action), (Kāya-kamma).
(4.) Lying is evil. (5.) Slandering is evil. (6.) Using harsh language is evil. (7.) Vain talk is evil.	II. Verbal Action, (Vacī-kamma).
(8.) Covetousness is evil.[19] (9.) Cruelty is evil.[20] (10.) Harmful views (Micchā-ditthi) are evil.[21]	III. Mental Action (Mano-kamma).

And what, Brothers, is the root of Evil? Greed (Lobha) is the Root of Evil; anger (Dosa) is the Root of Evil; delusion (Moha) is the root of evil.[22]

---

17. "Akusala" every deed is called which has a pernicious effect upon our Kamma (existence) and which, in its working manifests itself as suffering either in this life or in future lives.

18. All intentional killing or hurting of living beings no matter upon what pretext, is to be looked upon as Akusala.

19. "Whatsoever another possesses of wealth and riches,—to covet the same, thus; 'Ah! If only this were mine, which belongs to that other'" (Commentary.)

20. "Namely, the thought: 'These beings ought to be killed, slain, destroyed; they ought to perish.'" (Commentary.)

21. "The views: 'Alms and gifts are a vain delusion; there is neither reward nor recompence of good or of evil action, and so forth.'" (Commentary.)

22. The arising of Lobha as well as of Dosa is always accompanied by Moha.

And what, Brothers, is Good (Kusala) ?

(1.)	To abstain from Killing is good.	
(2.)	To abstain from Stealing is good.	I. Bodily Action (Kāya-kamma.)
(3.)	To abstain from Unlawful sexual Intercourse is good.	
(4.)	To abstain from Lying is good.	
(5.)	To abstain from Slandering is good.	II. Verbal Action (Vaci-kamma.)
(6.)	To abstain from Harsh Language is good.	
(7.)	To abstain from Vain Talk is good.	
(8.)	To be free from Covetousness is good.	
(9.)	To be free from Cruelty is good.	III. Mental Action (Mano-kamma.)
(10.)	Right Understanding (Sammā-diṭṭhi) is good.	

And what, Brothers, is the Root of Good? Freedom from Greed (Alobha) is the Root of Good ; freedom from Anger (Adosa) is the Root of Good ; freedom from Delusion (Amoha) is the Root of Good.

Understanding of the Truth of Suffering. And further, Brothers, when the disciple understands Suffering and the Cause of Suffering ; when he understands the Cessation of Suffering and the Path that leads to the Cessation of Suffering ; this, Brothers, is Right Understanding.[23]

Unprofitable Questions. But should anyone say: I am not willing to lead the disciple's life under the Blessed One unless the Blessed One first tells me whether the world is eternal or temporal ; whether the world is finite or infinite ; whether the personality is identical with the body, or whether the personality is one thing

---

23. There are two kinds of Right Understanding, namely, the mundane (Lokya-sammādiṭṭhi), and the ultra-mundane (Lokuttara-sammādiṭṭhi). The latter is possessed only by the members of the Four Degrees of Holy Disciples ; that is, by those who have realized one of the four ultra-mundane paths ;—that of the Sotāpanna, the Sakadāgāmi, the Anāgāmi, or the Arahaṁ. (See Note 25.)

and the body another ; whether the Perfect One continues
to exist after death or does not continue to exist after death
such an one, Brothers, would die ere the Perfect One could
tell him all this.

It is, Brothers, as if a man were pierced through by a
poisoned arrow, and his friends, companions and near relatives called in a surgeon, and he should say "I will not
have this arrow pulled out until I know who the man is that
has wounded me ; whether he is of the royal caste or the
priest's caste, a citizen or a servant ;" or else he should say :
"I will not have this arrow pulled out until I know who the
man is that has wounded me ; what is his name and to
what family he belongs" ; or else he should say :" I will not
have this arrow pulled out until I know who the man is
that has wounded me, whether he is tall or short, or of
medium height" ; verily, Brothers, such an one would die ere
he could sufficiently get to know all this.

O that the man who seeks his own welfare might pull
out this arrow,—this arrow of lamentation, of pain and of
sorrow ; for, whether these theses exist or not : 'The world
is eternal,' 'The world is temporal,' 'The world is finite,'
'The world is infinite,' certainly there is birth, there is decay,
there is death, sorrow, lamentation, suffering, grief, and
despair, the cessation of which, attainable even in this present life, I make known unto you.

There is for instance, Brothers, an unlearned, a common
man void of regard for holy men, without knowledge of the
teaching of holy men, untrained in the discipline of holy men,
void of regard for the good, without knowledge of the good,
untrained in the good.

He is possessed by the Self-illusion (Sakkāyadiṭṭhi) ;[24]
his heart is deluded by Scepticism, by
The Five Fetters. Faith in Ceremonialism, Lust and Anger ;
and how one can free one's self from these Fetters,—this
he does not really know, and to him these evils become
fetters that bind him to lower existence (i.e., to the sensuous universe,) because he has allowed them to become
strong and has not subdued them.

---

24. The Self-illusion (Sakkāya-diṭṭhi may reveal itself as :—
     (1) Materialism (Uccheda or Vibhava-diṭṭhi, literally, the Belief in
         Annihilation) or more fully stated, the belief that this visible
         material existence forms an I-being which is annihilated at
         the death of the material body ; or else as :
     (2) Spiritualism (Sassata-or Bhava-diṭṭhi, literally, Eternalism), that
         is to say, the belief in an I-being existing independently of
         the material body, and continuing to exist even after the
         dissolution of the latter.

Unacquainted with the things worthy of consideration, unacquainted with the things unworthy of consideration, he considers the unworthy and not the worthy.

And unwisely he considers thus: "Have I been in the past? Or have I not been? What have I **The Sixteen** been in the past? From what state, and **Doubts concern-** into what state, did I change in the past? **ing Past,Present** Shall I be in the future? Or shall I not be? **and Future.** What shall I be in the future? From what state and into what state shall I change in the future?"

And the present also fills him with doubt: "Am I then? Or am I not? What am I? In what way am I? This present being, whence has it come? And whither will it go?"

And with such unwise considerations, he falls into one or other of the Six Views: 'I have an **The Six Views** eternal self (Attā),' becomes his conviction **about the Soul.** and his firm view, or: 'I have no eternal self,' becomes his conviction and his firm view, or: 'With the absolute Self, I perceive the absolute Self (Attā) ' becomes his conviction and his firm view, or: 'With the absolute Self I perceive the relative self (Anattā),' becomes his conviction and his firm view, or: 'With the absolute Self I perceive the relative self (Anatta)' becomes his conviction and his firm view, or: 'With the relative self (Anattā) I perceive the absolute Self,' becomes his conviction and his firm view, or he falls into the following view: 'This my Self is to be found again when it enjoys here and there, in this or the other place, the reward of good and evil deeds, and this my Self is permanent, persistent, eternal, and, not subject to change, shall thus eternally remain the same.' Is not this, Brothers, really a doctrine of fools? These, Brothers, are mere views, they are snare of views, a labyrinth of views, a puppet-show of views, a moil of views, a tangle of views, and entangled in views, Brothers, the worldling, ignorant of the truth, will not be freed from re-birth, from decay and from death, from sorrow, lamentation, suffering grief, and despair; he will not be freed, I say, from suffering.

The holy disciple however, Brothers, who is acquainted with the truth, has regard for holy men, knows the teaching of holy men, is well-trained in the discipline of holy men, has regard for the good, knows the good, is well-trained in the good. He understands what is worthy of consideration and understands what is unworthy of consideration. Ac-

quainted with worthy things, acquainted with unworthy
things, he has no regard for unworthy things but has regard
for the worthy. " This is Suffering," he wisely considers.
" This is the Cause of Suffering," he wisely considers.
" This is the Cessation of Suffering" he wisely considers.
" This is the Path that leads to the Cessation of Suffering,"
he wisely considers. And by such wise considerations he is released from three fetters :—Self-illusion,[25]
" Hearership "
(Sotapatti.)
Scepticism, and Faith in Ceremonialism,
and those disciples, who are freed from these
three Fetters,—all these have become " Hearers of the
Message" (Sotāpannā), have for ever escaped the states of
torment and are assured of complete enlightenment. Hence
also it is said :—

" More than any earthly power,
" More than all the joys of heaven,
" More than rule o'er all the worlds,
" Is the fruit of ' Hearership.'

If, Brothers, one should put the question: ' Does the
Master Gotama admit any view at all ?' then such an one
is to be answered thus:

" The Tathāgata, Brothers, is free from any theory ; for
the Tathāgata, Brothers, has seen : ' Thus
Free from all
Theories.
is the Body, thus it arises, thus it passes
away ; thus is Sensation, thus it arises, thus
it passes away ; thus is Perception, thus it arises, thus it
passes away ; thus are the Subjective Differentiations (mental
properties), thus they arise, thus they pass away ; thus is
consciousness, thus it arises, thus it passes away !' Therefore, I say, the Tathāgata has won complete deliverance
through the annihilation, alienation, cessation, rejection,
and getting rid of all opinions and conjectures, of all self-
hood, self-seeking and vainglory.

---

25. There are Ten Fetters (Saññojanas) in all, which bind beings to existence. They are:—(1) *Self*-illusion (See previous note.) (2) Doubt. (3)
Faith in Ceremonialism. (4) Sensual Craving, (Kāma-rāga.) (5) Anger.
(6) Craving for Existence in the sphere of pure form *i.e.*, free from Kāma or
sensuality. (7) Craving for Formless Existence. (8) Pride. (9) Restlessness (in concentration.) (10) Illusion (Avijjā.) A Sotāpanna or ' Hearer '
is one who is free from the first three Fetters. He who has overcome the
fourth and the fifth Fetters in their grosser form is called Sakadāgāmi, or
' Once-returner ' to the sensuous sphere. Whoso is wholly freed from the
first five Fetters, which bind to existence in the sensual sphere is an Anagāmi
or ' Non-returner '; he can never again be born in the sensual sphere, since
all his sensual craving is for ever extinguished· Such an one realises Nibbāna, reaching it directly from the Rupaloka or sphere of pure form. The
one who is free from all the ten fetters is called an Arahaṁ or Perfectly
Holy One.

And whether, Brothers, Tathāgatas appear in the
world or whether Tathāgatas do not appear
in the world, it still remains a fact and a
fixed and necessary condition, that all things
are transient; for the Body is transient,
Sensation is transient, Perception is tran-
sient, the Subjective Differentiations are transient, Consciousness is transient.

The three Marks of Exis-tence.
1. Transiency. (Anicca).

Whether, Brothers, Tathāgatas appear in the world or
whether Tathagatas do not appear in the
world, it still remains a fact and a fixed and
necessary condition, that all things are sub-
ject to suffering; for the Body is subject to suffering, Sensation is subject to suffering, Perception is subject to suffering, the Subjective Differentiations are subject to suffering,
Consciousness is subject to suffering.

2. Suffering (Dukkha).

Whether, Brothers, Tathāgatas appear in the world or
whether Tathāgatas do not appear in the
world, it still remains a fact and a fixed and
necessary condition, that nothing whatso-
ever constitutes an individuality (Attā); for, the Body is not
individual (Anattā), Sensation is not individual, Perception
is not individual, the Subjective Differentiations are not individual, Consciousness is not individual.

3. Unsub-stantiality. (Anatta).

A body, a sensation, a perception, a subjective differen-
tiation, a consciousness, Brothers, that were permanent and
persistent, eternal and not subject to change,—this, the
wise declare, does not exist in the world. And it is not
possible that a being possessed of Right Understanding
should regard anything as an individual.

If, Brothers, someone should say: 'Sensation is my
absolute Self (Attā)' he should be answered
thus: "There are, Brothers, three kinds of
sensation,—pleasureable sensation, painful
sensation, and neutral sensation. Which of these three sensations now, do you consider to be your absolute Self? At
the moment when a man experiences one of these sensations,
he does not experience the other two. These three kinds of
sensation are called transient, conditioned by causes; they
are subject to decay, to dissolution; for their being consists
in separation, in passing away. Whoso in experiencing one
of these three sensations should speak thus: 'This is my
Self,'—he ought also to say then: 'My Self expires through

Discussions concerning the Self.

the disappearance of this sensation,' and doing so, he at that moment also acknowledges his own Self to be transient in this life.

If, Brothers, any one should say : ' Sensation is not my absolute Self, my absolute Self is inaccessible to sensation, he should be answered thus : " If, Brother, there were no sensation present in you, would you then say ' I am ' ? Surely not, Brother ! " Accordingly it would be entirely absurd to share such an opinion with him.

If, Brothers, anyone should say : " Sensation is not my absolute Self but it is false to maintain that my absolute Self is inaccessible to sensation ; it is my absolute Self that experiences sensation, for feeling is a faculty of my absolute Self," he should be answered thus : " If sensation Brother, should come to total annihilation, without leaving a single trace behind, and if thus no sensation whatever were to be found, could you then say, following upon the non-existence of sensation : ' I am ' ? Surely not, Brother ! " Accordingly it would be entirely absurd to share such an opinion with him.

' Thoughts are the absolute Self,'—such an assertion is entirely devoid of foundation ; for, in all thinking an arising and a passing away are seen and if an arising and a passing away are there seen, the thesis : ' My Self arises and passes away ' must as a consequence hold good ; hence it is not proper to maintain ' Thoughts are the absolute Self ;' accordingly thoughts are not a Self.

' Thought-consciousness is the absolute Self '—such an assertion is entirely devoid of foundation ; for in thought-consciousness an arising and a passing away are seen, and if an arising and a passing away are there seen, the thesis : ' My Self arises and passes away,' must as a consequence hold good ; hence it is not proper to maintain : ' Thought-consciousness is the absolute Self ;' accordingly thought-consciousness is not a Self.

' The mind is the absolute Self,'—such an assertion is entirely devoid of foundation ; for in the mind, an arising and a passing away are seen, and if an arising and a passing away are there seen, the thesis : ' My Self arises and passes away,' must hold good as a consequence ; hence it is not proper to maintain : ' The mind is the absolute Self ;' accordingly the mind is not a Self.

Surely, Brothers, it would be more correct to say that

The Body is more constant than the Mind. the body (Rūpa) formed out of the four elementary powers is a self, instead of these subjective aspects (Nāma), for it is evident that this body, built up out of the Four Elementary Forces, lasts for a year, for two years, for three, four, five, six, or even for seven years; but that which is called mind, understanding, or consciousness, is found day and night in a state of incessant change, passing away as one thing, and returning as another thing.[26]

Therefore, Brothers, whatsoever there is of Material Existence, of Sensation, of Perception, of Subjective Differentiations, of Consciousness, whether one's own or another's, gross or refined, lofty or low, far or near, there one should recognise according to reality and true wisdom : "This does not belong to me ; this am I not ; this is no ' I ' (Anattā)."

If now, Brothers, anyone should ask you; ' Have you

Past, Present, Future. been in the past or have you not been ? will you be in the future or will you not be ? Are you or are you not ?', you ought to say that in one respect you have been in the past, but that yet in another respect you had not been; that in one respect you will be in the future but that yet in another respect you will not be ; that in one respect you are, but that yet in another respect you are not.

Verily, only he who perceives Origination from Causes, perceives the truth : and he who perceives the truth, perceives Origination from Causes. For, Brothers, just as milk comes from the cow, and cream originates from milk, butter from cream, and cheese from butter ;—and when it is milk it is not called cream, nor butter, nor cheese ; and when it is cheese, the same is not designated by any other name ; even so, Brothers, when one of the three kinds of existence (past, present, or future existence) is represented, this is not designated by the names of either of the other two ; these, Brothers, are merely names, merely manners of speaking, designations in common conversational use. The Blessed One indeed, makes use of these, without however being led astray by them.

---

26. " Strictly speaking, the existence of a being is extremely brief and lasts only during the interval of a single thought. So soon as the thought ends, the being also ends; for ;—
" The being of the future moment will live in the future, but has not lived in the past, nor does it yet live now.
The being of the present moment lives just now, but has not lived in the past, nor will it live in the future."

Verily, Brothers, if we hold the view that we are identical with our Material Existence,—in that
case a holy life is not possible ; or if, Brothers, we hold the view good that there is
an absolute Self (The ' Soul'), independent
of this body,—in this case also a holy life is
not possible. (Cf. Notes 11 and 24.)

The two Extremes, (Materialism—Spiritualism) and the Middle Doctrine.

But these two extremes are both rejected by the Exalted
One, and there is a Middle Doctrine which teaches:

On *Delusion* depends self-affirming *Action* (*i.e.* bodily,
verbal and mental kusala-akusala-Kamma. See page 100.)
On self-affirming Action depends the arising of (rebirth)
Consciousness (*i.e.* conception in the womb of the mother.)
On the arising of Consciousness depends the *Subjective*
(mental)-*Objective* (material) *Aspects of Existence.* On the
Subjective-Objective Aspects of Existence depends the six-
fold activity of the *Senses.* On the Senses depends *Contact*
(with the objectively perceived objects of Sense :—forms,
sounds, odours, tastes, bodily touches, ideas.) On Contact
depends the six-fold pleasant, painful or neutral *Sensations.*
On Sensation depends *Craving* (Taṇhā.) On Craving depends *Clinging to Existence.* On Clinging to Existence depends the *Process of Becoming.* On the Process of Becoming (self-affirming) Action) depends (future) *Birth.* On
Birth depends decay and death, sorrow, lamentation, suffering, grief and despair. Thus arises the whole mass of Suffering. (Cf. The Second Truth p. 11.)

Through the complete fading out and cessation of
Delusion (Avijjā), self-affirming Action is done away.
Through the cessation of self-affirming Action, Consciousness (re-birth) is done away ; through the cessation of consciousness, the Subjective-Objective Aspects of Existence are
done away ; through the cessation of the subjective-objective
aspects of existence, the six-fold activity of the Senses is done
away ; through the cessation of the six-fold activity of the
senses, Contact (of the sense-organs with the objectively perceived world) is done away ; through the cessation of contact,
Sensation is done away ; through the cessation of sensation,
Craving is done away ; through the cessation of craving,
Clinging to Existence is done away ; through the cessation
of clinging to existence, the Process of Becoming is done
away ; through the cessation of the process of becoming
(self-affirming Action), Re-birth is done away ; through not
being re-born, decay and death sorrow, lamentation, suffer-

ing, grief and despair are done away. Thus ceases the whole mass of suffering. (Cf. The Third Truth p. 15.)

Verily, Brothers, because beings buried in Delusion seized by Craving, now here, now there, seek ever fresh delight,—therefore is it that there comes about ever fresh Re-birth ; and the Action (Kamma) of men, that is done out of Greed (Lobha) Anger (Dosa), or Delusion (Moha), which springs out of greed, anger, or delusion, which is brought about by them, which has its origin in them, ripens wheresoever there are men ; and wheresoever that action ripens even there does man earn the Fruit of his Action, be it in this or in some future life. (Cf. Note 9.)

Effective Kamma.

However, Brothers through the complete fading out of delusion, through the arising of Wisdom, through the annihilation of Craving(Taṇhā,) no future birth lies any more before ; for the Actions (Kamma)of men, Brothers, that are not dueto Greed, Anger, or Delusion, which do not spring from greed, anger, or delusion, which are not brought about by them, which have not their origin in them, in as much as greed, hate, and anger have disappeared, have been abandoned and rooted out, such actions like a palm tree torn out of the soil are cut off and do not lead to any further entry into existence.

Barren Kamma.

In this respect, Brothers, verily one may rightly say of me "The ascetic Gotama teaches negation, the ascetic Gotama teaches annihilation," for certainly, Brothers, I teach annihilation—the Annihilation namely, of Greed, the Annihilation of Anger, the Annihilation of Delusion, as well as the Annihilation of the manifold evil, unwholesome conditions of the mind. (Cf. Note 9.)

THE SECOND LINK OF THE PATH.

RIGHT MINDEDNESS SAMMA-SANKAPPA.

What now Brothers, is Right Mindedness ?

The three-fold intention.

1. The thought of renouncing worldly ways.
2. The thought of bearing no ill-will.
3. The thought of abstaining from cruelty.

This, Brothers, is Right Mindedness.

Renunciation of the world.

Thus for example, a householder or the son of a householder, or some other man, hears the teaching of the Perfect One.

After he has heard this teaching he is filled with confidence in the Perfect One. And filled with this confidence, he thinks : "A prison house is household life, a refuse heap : but pilgrim-life is as the open air. Not easy is it when one lives at home, to fulfil point by point the rules of the holy life. How if now, with hair and beard cut off, clothed in the yellow robe,---how if I go forth from home to the homeless life ? " And in a short time, having given up his more or less extensive possessions, having forsaken a smaller or larger circle of relations, he cuts off hair and beard, puts on the yellow robe and goes forth from home to the homeless life.

THE THIRD LINK OF THE PATH.

RIGHT SPEECH, SAMMA-VACA.

What now Brothers, is Right Speech ?

1. A man, Brothers, has overcome lying and he
Abstaining from Lying. abstains from telling falsehood. He speaks the truth, he is devoted to the truth, he adheres to the truth, he is worthy of confidence, is not a deceiver of men. Coming now amongst people or amongst relatives, or into a meeting, or being brought before a judge and asked to give his testimony :' ' Come, good man tell what thou knowest ' he answers, if he knows nothing : 'I know nothing,' and if he knows, he answers : ' I know '; if he has seen nothing he answers : ' I have seen nothing,' and if he has seen, he answers : ' I have seen.' Thus he never knowingly speaks a lie, neither for the sake of his own advantage, nor for the sake of another person's advantage nor for the sake of any advantage whatsoever.

2. He has overcome Slandering, he abstains from abuse.
Abstaining from Slandering. What he has heard here, he does not repeat there, so as to cause dissension there, and what he has heard there, he does not repeat here, so as to cause dissension here. Thus he brings together those that are at variance ; establishes those that are united ; concord makes him glad ; he delight in concord ; it is concord that he spreads by his words.

He has given up Harsh Language, he abstains from
Abstaining from Harsh Language. Harsh Language. He speaks words that are free from rudeness, soothing to the ear, loving, going to the heart, courteous, rejoicing many, elevating many. He knows : " In whom the thought dwells, ' He has slandered me, beaten me ; he has overpowered me and robbed me,' such an one never gets free from hate ; for hatred never ceases by hatred ; by love alone is it removed ; this is an eternal law."

And he remembers the worlds of the Blessed One : " Even, Brothers, should robbers and murderers saw off your limbs and joints, whoso gave way to anger thereat, would not be following my advice. For thus, Brothers, ought you to train yourselves : ' Undisturbed shall our mind remain, no evil words shall escape our lips ; friendly and full of sympathy shall we remain, with heart full of love and free from any hidden malice ; and that person shall we penetrate with loving thoughts, wide, deep, boundless, freed from anger and hatred.' Thus brothers, ought you to train yourselves."

4. He has overcome vain talk and he abstains from vain talk. He speaks at the right time, speaks in accordance with facts, speaks to the point. He speaks about the Truth (Dhamma) and the Discipline of the Order (Vinaya) ; his speech is of real value and agrees with its object ; for he bears in mind the injunction which says : " In meeting one another, Brothers, there are two things that ought to be adhered to ; either conversation about the Truth or holy silence."

Abstaining from Vain Talk.

This, Brothers, is Right Speech.

THE FOURTH LINK OF THE PATH.

RIGHT ACTION, SAMMA-KAMMANTA.

What now Brothers, is Right Action ?

Abstaining from Killing. A man Brothers, has given up Killing, abstains from Killing. Without stick or sword, compassionate, full of sympathy, he cherishes kindness and pity for all living beings.

Abstaining from Stealing. 2. He has given up Stealing, he abstains from Stealing. He takes what is given him ; he waits for what is given him ; free from thievish thoughts, with heart purified.

Abstaining from unlawful Sexual Intercourse. Unlawful Sexual Intercourse he has given up ; he abstains from Unlawful Sexual Intercourse. He has no intercourse with maidens who are under the protection of father, mother, elders, brother, sister, or relatives, nor with married women nor with slaves, down to flower-decked dancing girls.

This Brothers, is Right Action.

THE FIFTH LINK OF THE PATH.

RIGHT LIVING, SAMMA-AJIVA.

What now, Brothers, is Right Living ?

When Brothers, the noble disciple, renouncing a wrong living, gets his livelihood by a right way of living,—this, Brothers, is Right Living.[27]

---

27. Amongst trades, there are five, which, being causes of misery to the world, are reckoned under Wrong Living ; they are :—
    (1) The trade of butchering and of dealing in butchered animals ;
        (also the occupations of hunter, fisherman, soldier, etc.)
    (2) Dealing in intoxicating drinks.
    (3) Dealing in poisons.
    (4) Dealing in arms and deadly weapons.
    (5) Dealing in human beings, as slaves, prostitutes, and so forth.
  To Wrong Living belong also the practices of deceit, treachery, soothsaying, trickery and usury.

THE SIXTH LINK OF THE PATH.

RIGHT EFFORT, SAMMA-VAYAMA.

What now, Brothers, is Right Effort?

There are, Brothers, Four Great Efforts: The Effort to Avoid, the Effort to Overcome, the Effort to Originate, and the Effort to Maintain.

1. What now, Brothers, is the Effort to Avoid?

The Effort to Avoid (Samvara-ppadhana.) The disciple, Brothers, begets in himself the will not to permit to arise evil unwholesome things that have not arisen, and summoning all his strength, he struggles and strives and incites his mind.

When, Brothers, this disciple sees a form with the eye, hears a sound with the ear, smells an odour with the nose, tastes a taste with the tongue feels a contact with the body, perceives an object (idea) with the mind, he does not indulge in the aspect of the same, neither of the whole nor of its parts; and he begets in himself the will to avoid that, which, if he remained with unguarded senses, would give occasion for the arising of evil things, of desire and discontent. And so, watching over the senses, he succeeds in becoming master of them. Possessed of this noble control over the senses, he experiences inwardly a feeling of joy into which no evil thing can enter. This, Brothers, is called the Effort to Avoid.

2. What now, Brothers, is the Effort to Overcome.

The Effort to Overcome. (Pahana-ppadhana.) The disciple, Brothers, begets in himself the will to overcome evil, unwholesome things that have arisen, and, summoning all his strength, he struggles and strives and incites his mind. He does not allow a thought of Greed, Anger or Delusion that has arisen, to find a foothold; he suppresses it, expels it, annihilates it, causes it to disappear. And whatsoever there is of evil, unwholesome things, he does not allow them to find a foothold, he overcomes them, expels them, annihilates them, causes them to disappear.

Five methods of expelling evil thoughts. If, Brothers, by the dwelling upon a certain idea, there arise in the disciple, evil, unwholesome thoughts, of Greed, Anger, Delusion,—(1) then the disciple out of this idea should gain another and a wholesome idea, (2) or, he should dwell upon the misery of those thoughts, thus, 'There they are again, these unwholesome thoughts; there they are again, these pernicious thoughts; there they are again, these pain-producing thoughts.' (3) Or he should pay no attention to them. (4) Or he should analyse them into their constituent parts. (5) Or, with teeth clenched and tongue pressed against the gums, he should suppress these thoughts with his mind ; and in doing so, these evil, unwholesome thoughts of Greed, Anger, or Delusion, will dissolve and disappear, and the mind will become settled and quiet, concentrated and strong.

This, Brothers, is called the Effort to Overcome.

3. What now, Brothers is the Effort to Originate ?

The disciple, Brothers, begets in himself the will to originate wholesome things that have not **The Effort to Originate. (Bhavana-ppadhana).** arisen, and summoning all his strength, he struggles and strives and incites his mind.

And he originates the Constituent Parts of Enlightenment (Bojjhanga) born of solitude, depending upon detachment, connected with extinction, and leading to relinquishment,—namely, Attentiveness, Penetration (Dhammavicaya), Energy, Joy, Tranquility, Concentration (Samādhi) and Equanimity.[28]

This, Brothers, is called the Effort to Originate.

4. What now, Brothers, is called the Effort to Maintain? The disciple, Brothers, begets in **The Effort to Maintain.** himself the will to maintain wholesome things that have arisen, the will not to permit them to perish but to bring them to perfection; and summoning all his strength, he struggles and strives and incites his mind.

This, Brothers, is called the Effort to Maintain.

Such a disciple, Brothers, is vigorous and alert; his energies are equally balanced, neither too ardent nor too sluggish in pursuing the Middle Path. And he is filled with the thought : ' May muscles, skin and sinews, together with bones, flesh, and blood, shrivel together and dry up, rather than that I should abandon my efforts while as yet I have not attained whatsoever is attainable by human perseverance, energy, and endeavour.'

This, Brothers, is Right Effort.

---

28. The Bojjhangas are also possessed in some degree by the Puthujjana or Worldling, that is, by one, who is still outside the four Ultramundane Paths (of the Sotāpanna, Sakadāgāmi, etc.)

THE SEVENTH LINK OF THE PATH.

RIGHT ATTENTIVENESS, SAMMA-SATI.

What now, Brothers, is Right Attentiveness?

The disciple, Brothers, lives in Contemplation of the **The Four Satipatthanas or Fundamentals of Attentiveness.** Body, lives in Contemplation of the Sensations, lives in Contemplation of the Mind, lives in Contemplation of Internal Phenomena, unweariedly, clearly conscious, with senses awake, having overcome worldly desires and sorrows.

The only way, Brothers, that leads mortals to the attainment of purity, to the overcoming of sorrow and lamentation, to the cessation of suffering and grief, to the entering upon the right path and the realisation of Nibbāna, is the " Four Fundamentals of Attentiveness," the Four Satipaṭṭhānas.

1. THE CONTEMPLATION OF THE BODY, (KAYA).[29]

But how, Brothers, does the disciple dwell in the Contemplation of the Body?

The disciple, Brothers, retires to the forest, to the foot of a tree or to a solitary place, sits himself down with legs crossed, body erect, and mind present and fixed.

With attentive mind he breathes in, with attentive **Anapana sati or " Watching over In and Out-breathing."** mind he breathes out. When he takes a long inward breath, he knows: ' I take a long inward breath '; when he makes a long outward breath, he knows : ' I make a long outward breath '; when he makes a short inward breath, he knows : ' I take a short inward breath;' when he makes a short outward breath, he knows : ' I make a short outward breath.' ' Clearly perceiving the entire breath, I will breathe in ;' thus he trains himself; ' Clearly perceiving the entire breath, I will breathe out ' thus he trains himself. ' Calm-

---

29. Kâva—here. Rūpa-kāya—constitutes the Rūpa-khandha or Aspect of Material Existence.

ing the breath, I will breathe in,' thus he trains himself ;
' Calming the breath, I will breathe out,' thus he trains
himself.[30]

Thus he contemplates his own Body ;[31] thus he contemplates the Bodies of others ; thus he contemplates both
his own Body and the Bodies of others. He beholds how
Bodies arises ; beholds how Bodies passes away ; beholds
the arising and the passing away of Bodies. ' Bodies only
are there ':[32] this clear knowledge is present to him, just
because he possesses understanding, possesses insight, and
he lives independent, unattached to anything in the world.
Thus, Brothers, does the disciple dwell in Contemplation
of the Body.

And further, Brothers, the disciple knows in going,
standing, sitting and lying down, how one

**Insight into
the Four Posi-
tions of the Body.** has to understand according to truth ' I go,'
' I stand,' ' I sit,' ' I lie down,' ' I find
myself in this or the other position.'[33]

Thus he contemplates his own Body ; thus he contemplates the Bodies of others ; thus he contemplates both his
own Body and the Bodies of others. He beholds how
Bodies arise ; beholds how Bodies pass away ; beholds the
arising and the passing away of Bodies. ' Bodies only are
there ': this clear knowledge is present to him, just because

---

30. After the disciple through Watching over In and Out-breathing,
has attained the Four Jhānas or Trances (See The Eighth Link of the
Path), he considers in his mind as to what In and Out-breathing is
based upon, and he understands : ' In-and Out-breathing presuppose the existence of the body.' The body however, is only a name for the Four Chief
Elements and the properties dependent upon them, namely,(Eye, Ear, Nose,
Tongue, Body, Form, Sound, Odour, Taste, etc., (See Note, 5). Dependent upon the contact of these, consciousness (Viññāna) arises ; and through
consciousness there arise all the five Aspects of Existence, namely, the
Mental Aspects (Nāma) : Sensation, Perception, Subjective Differentiations,
and Consciousness, and the Material Aspect (Rūpa) ; all which, taken together, constitute the subjective-objective *Anschauung* (Nāma-rūpa).'
    Here the disciple clearly perceives : ' There is no being present, but
only the Five Khandhas or Aspects of Existence whose arising is dependent upon causes ;' and in the moment of deep Insight (Vipassanā) into the
Transiency, Suffering, and Unsubstantiality (Anattā) of all that has thus
arisen, he may realise any one of the Four Ultramundane Paths ; in other
words, enter into Sotāpanna-ship, Sakadāgāmi-ship, Anāgāmi-ship or
Arahatship. (Cf. Note, 50.)
    31. " By body in this case is meant breath, the latter being a Kāya-
saṅkhāra or bodily function."
(Commentary.)
    32. " This is only a material body ; it is no living being, no individual,
no woman, no man, no self, nothing that belongs to a self ; neither a person
nor anything belonging to a person."
(Commentary.)
    33 " The disciple understands that there is no living being, no real
that goes, stands, sits, or lies down, but that it is by a mere figure of speech
that one says : ' I go,' ' I stand,' and so forth."
(Commentary.)

he possesses understanding, possesses insight, and he lives independent, unattached to anything in the world. Thus, Brothers, does the disciple dwell in Contemplation of the Body.

And further still, Brothers, the disciple is clearly conscious in his coming and going, clearly conscious in directing his eyes towards an object and in turning away his eyes, clearly conscious in bending and in straightening any part of his body, clearly conscious in eating, drinking, chewing and tasting ; clearly conscious in evacuating excrement and urine ; clearly conscious in walking, standing and sitting ; clearly conscious in falling asleep and in awakening ; clearly conscious in speaking and in keeping silence. 34

The Four-fold Clear Consciousness.

Thus he contemplates his own Body ; thus he contemplates the Bodies of others ; thus he contemplates both his own Body and the Bodies of others. He beholds how Bodies arise ; beholds how Bodies pass away ; beholds the arising, and the passing away of Bodies. ' Bodies only are there ': this clear knowledge is present to him, just because he possesses understanding, possesses insight, and he lives independent, unattached to anything in the world. Thus, Brothers, does the disciple dwell in Contemplation of the Body.

And further still, Brothers, the disciple contemplates this Body up and down from the sole of the foot to the crown of the head, a skin drawn over it, filled with manifold impurities : ' This Body has hair on the head, is covered with hair, has nails and teeth, skin and flesh, sinews, bones and marrow, kidneys, heart, and liver, diaphragm, spleen, lungs, stomach, bowels, mesentery and excrement ; has bile, phlegm, pus, blood, sweat, lymph, tears, sperm, spittle, nasal mucus, oil of the joints, and urine.'

Contemplation on the Impurity of the Body.

Just, Brothers, as if there were a sack, tied up at both ends, filled with all kinds of grain,—with rice, beans, sesamum,—and a man not blind opened it and investigated its contents, thus : ' That is rice these are beans, this is sesamum ' :—just so Brothers, does the disciple consider this body from the sole of the feet to the crown of the head, skin drawn over it, filled with manifold impurities.

---

34. " In all that the disciple is doing he is clearly conscious : (1) of his Intention, (2) of his Advantage, (3) of his Duty, 4) of the Reality."
(Commentary.)

And further still, Brothers, the disciple contemplates on
this Body as it goes and stands, as analysed
**The Analysis
of the Body.** into its Elements: 'This Body is put together out of the Solid Element (Pathavi-
dhātu), the Liquid Element (Apo-dhātu), the Heating Element (Tejo-dhātu), and the Vibrating Element (Vāyo-dhātu).
(Cf. ' The Four Chief Elements.' Page, 5.)

Exactly Brothers, as a skilled butcher or butcher's ap-
prentice might slaughter a cow, bring it to market, divide
it into separate portions, and sit himself down; just so Brothers, does the disciple contemplate on this Body as analysed into its Elements.

Thus he contemplates his own Body; thus he contemplates the Bodies of others; thus he contemplates both his
own Body and the Bodies of others. He beholds how Bodies
arise; beholds how Bodies pass away; beholds the arising
and the passing away of Bodies. ' Bodies only are there ':
this clear knowledge is present to him, just because he
possesses understanding, possesses insight, and he lives independent, unattached to anything in the world. Thus,
Brothers, does the disciple dwell in Contemplation of the
Body.

1. And further still, Brothers; just as if the disciple
should see a corpse lying in the burial-
**The Cemetery
Meditations.** ground, one day dead, or two or three days.
dead, swollen up, blue-black in colour, a
prey to corruption,—he concludes as regards himself, ' And
my Body also shall so become, has a like destiny, cannot
escape it.'

2. And further still, Brothers, just as if the disciple
should see a corpse lying in the burial-ground, picked to
pieces by crows, or ravens, or vultures, stripped of its flesh
by dogs or jackals, or gnawed by all kinds of worms,—he
concludes as regards himself, ' And my Body also shall so
become, has a like destiny, cannot escape it.'

3. And further still, Brothers, just as if the disciple
should see a corpse lying in the burial-ground, a framework
of bones, flesh hanging from it, bespattered with blood, held
together by the sinews, or,

4.—a framework of bones, stripped of flesh, bespattered
with blood, held together by the sinews, or,

5.—a framework of bones, without flesh, without blood,
held together by its sinews or,

6.—the bones, without the sinews, scattered hither and thither ; here a bone of the hand, there a bone of the foot, there a shin bone, there a thigh bone, there the pelvis, there the spine, there the skull,—when he beholds this, he concludes as regards himself : ' And my body also shall so become, has a like destiny, cannot escape it.'

7. And further still, Brothers, the disciple should see a corpse lying in the burial-ground, bones white and of the colour of shells, or,

8.—bones, heaped together after the lapse of a year, or,

9.—bones, weathered away, and crumbled to dust,— he concludes as regards himself : ' And my Body also shall so become, has a like destiny, cannot escape it.'

Thus he contemplates his own Body ; thus he contemplates the Bodies of others ; thus he contemplates both his own Body and the Bodies of others. He beholds how Bodies arise ; beholds how Bodies pass away ; beholds the arising and the passing away of Bodies. ' Bodies only are there ' : this clear knowledge is present to him, just because he possesses understanding, possesses insight, and he lives independent, unattached to anything in the world. Thus, Brothers, does the disciple dwell in Contemplation of the Body.[35]

If, Brothers, one has carried out and practised this Contemplation of the Body, applied himself to it, realised it, penetrated it deeply and brought it to perfection one may gain ten useful qualities.

The Fruits attained by the Contemplation of the Body.

Over Discontent one has mastery ; one does not allow one's self to be overcome by discontent ; one subdues and masters what discontent may have arisen.

One conquers Fear and Anxiety ; one does not allow one's self to be overcome by fear and anxiety ; one subdues and masters fear and anxiety that may have arisen.

One endures cold and heat, hunger and thirst, wind and weather, flies and wasps and noxious creeping creatures, wicked and malicious speech ; bodily pains and sensations that attack one, severe, sharp, piercing, unpleasant, dangerous to life,—these one patiently endures.

35. Of the Contemplations of the Body, ' Insight into the Four Positions of the Body,' ' The Four-fold Clear Consciousness,' and the ' Analysis of the Body,' properly constitute part of the teaching of Paññâ. The ' Cemetery Meditations ' belong partly to Paññâ and partly to Samâdhi. (Cf. Sîla, Samâdhi, Paññâ, page, 17.)

The 'Four Jhānas or Trances, the mind-purifying, bestowing happiness even here,—these one can enjoy at will without difficulty, without effort.

The Six Abihnnas[36] or the Six-fold Knowledge :

One is enabled to produce Magical Effects.[37] Up to the Brahma worlds one has the body in his power.

1. The Magical Powers (Iddhi).
2. The Heavenly Ear.

With the Heavenly Ear, the purified, the supra-human one hears both kinds of sounds, the heavenly and the earthly, the distant and the near.

3. The Knowledge of the Mind of other beings.

With the mind one sees into the Hearts of Other Beings, of other persons.

4. The Memory of previous Existence.

One remembers many previous Forms of Existence ; first one life, then two lives, then many lives, with their characteristic signs, with their specific connections.

5. The Heavenly Eye.

With the Heavenly Eye, the purified, the supra-human, one sees beings disappear and reappear, the base and the noble, the beautiful and the ugly, the fortunate and the unfortunate ; one perceives how beings return according to their deeds.

6. The End of Illusion.

One can put an end to Illusion and manifest, realise, and attain, even in this life, the stainless Deliverance of the Mind, the Deliverance through Wisdom.[38]

2. CONTEMPLATION OF THE SENSATIONS
(VEDANA.)

But how, Brothers, does the disciple dwell in Contemplation of the Sensations ?

In experiencing Sensations[397] Brothers, the disciple understands according to truth the Agreeable Sensation,

---

36. It is only after the attainment of the four Jhānas that one may succeed in reaching the first five Abhiññās.

37. The 'Four Iddhipādas' or Bases for the Obtaining of Magical Powers are : Concentration of Will, of Effort, of Mind, and of Investigation.

38. The first five Abhiññās are Mundane (lokiya) Conditions ; the sixth Abhiññā however, is Ultramundane (lokuttara) and identical with Kilesaparinibbāna or Arahatship. (See Note, 13.)

39. Mental and bodily sensations may be agreeable, disagreeable, or neutral.

The sensations however which accompany eye-consciousness, ear-consciousness, olfactory-consciousness, and tongue-consciousness, are always neutral sensations.

the Disagreeable Sensation, or the Neutral Sensation; he understands according to truth, the mundane or the ultra-mundane Agreeable Sensation, the mundane or the ultra-mundane Disagreeable Sensation, the mundane or the ultra-mundane Neutral Sensation.[40]

Thus he contemplates his own Sensations; thus he contemplates the Sensation of others; thus he contemplates both his own Sensations and the Sensations of others. He beholds how Sensations arise; beholds how they pass away; beholds the arising and the passing away of Sensations. 'Sensations only are there': this clear knowledge is present to him just because he possesses understanding, possesses insight, and he lives independent, unattached to anything in the world. Thus, Brothers, does the disciple dwell in Contemplation of the Sensations.

CONTEMPLATION OF THE THOUGHTS (CITTA).[41]

But how, Brothers, does the disciple dwell in Contemplation of the Thoughts?

The disciple, Brothers, perceives as Thoughts arise— the thoughts of Greed, and the thoughts free from Greed, the thoughts of Anger, and the thoughts free from Anger; the thoughts of Delusion, and the thoughts free from Delusion; the concentrated thoughts, and the scattered thoughts; the low thoughts, and the lofty thoughts; the base thoughts, and the noble thoughts; the concentrated thoughts, and the fickle thoughts; the freed thoughts, and the fettered thoughts.

Thus, he contemplates his own Thoughts; thus he contemplates the Thoughts of others; thus he contemplates both his own Thoughts and the Thoughts of others. He beholds how Thoughts arise; beholds how Thoughts pass away; beholds the arising and the passing away of Thoughts. 'Thoughts only are there': this clear knowledge is present to him, just because he possesses understanding, possesses insight, and he lives independent, unattached to anything in the world.

Thus, Brothers, does the disciple dwell in Contemplation of the Thoughts.

40. "The disciple understands that the expression ' I feel ' has no validity except as a figure of common speech; he understands that in the absolute sense there is no being or individual present who experiences the sensation." (Commentary.)
41. The thoughts belong to the Viññāṇa-kkhandha or the Aspect of Consciousness.

4. CONTEMPLATION OF INTERNAL PHENOMENA (DHAMMA.)[42]

But how, Brothers, does the disciple dwell in Contemplation of Internal Phenomena?

The Five Hindrances or Nivaranas.

The disciple, Brothers, dwells in Contemplation of Internal Phenomena, namely of the 'Five Hindrances.'[43]

1. The disciple, Brothers, knows, when there is Lust in him, 'In me is Lust;' he knows, when there is no Lust in him, 'In me is no Lust.' He knows how Lust comes to arise; knows how the Lust is overcome; knows where the Lust that is overcome, disappears for ever.[44]

2. He knows, when there is Anger in him, 'In me is Anger;' he knows when there is no Anger in him, 'In me is no Anger.' He knows how Anger comes to arise; he knows how Anger is overcome; knows where the Anger that is overcome disappears for ever.

3. He knows, when there is Laxness in him, 'In me is laxness;' he knows when there is no laxness in him, 'In me is no Laxness.' He knows how Laxness comes to arise; knows how Laxness is overcome; knows where the Laxness that is overcome disappears for ever.

4. He knows when there is Restless Brooding (Uddhacca-kukkucca) in him, 'In me is Restless Brooding;' knows when there is no Restless Brooding in him, 'In me is no Restless Brooding.' He knows how Restless Brooding comes to arise; knows how Restless Brooding is overcome;

---

42. The Dhammas (Objects of the Mind: perceptions, ideas) belong to the Saññā-kkhandha and the Saṅkhāra-kkhandha, or the Aspects of Perception and of the Subjective Differentiations. Hence the Four Contemplations of the Seventh Link include the Five Aspects of Existence. The first Contemplation relates to Material Existence; the Second, to Sensation; the Third, to Consciousness; and the Fourth to Perception and to the Subjective Differentiations.

43. Sensuous Craving, Anger, Laxness, Restless Brooding, and Doubt, are called Hindrances because their presence at the time hinders entrance into the Jhānas or Trances.

44. Sensuous Craving (Kāma-cchanda) arises through unwise thinking on the agreeable and delightful, and may be suppressed by the following six methods: Fixing the mind upon an idea that arouses disgust; Meditation upon the impurities of the body (Asubhā-bhāvanā); Watching over the six doors of the senses; Moderation in eating; Cultivating friendship with the good; and right Instruction. Sensuous Craving is for ever destroyed upon entrance into Anāgāmiship. (See Note, 25.)

(After the Commentary)

knows where Restless Brooding that is overcome disappears. for ever.[45]

5. He knows, when there are Doubts in him, ' In me are Doubts,' he knows when there are no Doubts in him, ' In me are no Doubts.' He knows how Doubts come to arise ; knows how Doubts are overcome ; knows where Doubts that are overcome, disappear for ever.[46]

Thus he contemplates Internal Phenomena in himself ; thus he contemplates Internal Phenomena in others ; thus he contemplates Internal Phenomena both in himself and in others. He perceives how Internal Phenomena arise ; perceives how Internal Phenomena pass away ; perceives the arising and the passing away of Internal Phenomena. ' Internal Phenomena only are there' ; this clear knowledge is present to him, just because he possesses understanding, possesses insight, and he lives independent, unattached to anything in the world. Thus, Brothers, does the disciple dwell in Contemplation of Internal Phenomena, namely, of the Five Hindrances.

And further still, Brothers, the disciple dwells in Contemplation of Internal Phenomena, namely of the ' Five Aspects of Existence.' He **Five Khandhas or Aspects of Existence.** knows : Thus is the Body (Rūpa) ; thus does it arise; thus does it pass away. Thus is Sensation (Vedanā) ; thus does it arise ; thus does it pass away. Thus is Perception (Saññā) ; thus does it arise, thus does it pass away. Thus are the Subjective Differentiations (Saṅkhāras) ; thus do they arise ; thus do they pass away. Thus is Consciousness (Viññāṇa) ; thus does it arise, thus does it pass away.

And further still, Brothers, the disciple dwells in Contemplation of Internal Phenomena, namely, **The Six Subjective-objective Sense-Domains.** of the ' Six Subjective-Objective Sense-Domains.'

The disciple, Brother, knows the eye and knows forms ; and the fetter that arises in dependence on them, this also he knows. He knows how the fetter comes to arise, knows how the fetter is overcome and where it disappears for ever.

---

45. " Uddhacca (Restlessness in Concentration) is destroyed upon entrance into Arahatship ; Kukkucca (Remorse, Scruples) upon entrance into Anāgāmiship." (Commentary.)
46. " Doubts are destroyed upon entrance into Hearership." (Commentary.)

He knows ear and sounds, nose and odours, tongue and tastes, body and touches, mind and ideas ; and the fetter that arises in dependence on them,—this also he knows. He knows how the fetter comes to arise, knows how the fetter is overcome, and where it disappears for ever.[47]

And further still, Brothers, the disciple dwells in Contemplation of Internal Phenomena, namely, of the 'Seven Constituent Parts of Enlightenment.

The Seven Bojjhangas or Constituent Parts of Enlightenment.

The disciple, Brothers, knows when there is Attentiveness in him, when there is Penetration in him, when there is Energy in him, when there is Joy in him, when there is Tranquillity in him, when there is Concentration in him, when there is Equanimity in him : ' In me exists this quality ;' and when they are not in him : ' In me this quality does not exist.' He knows how the Constituent Parts of Enlightenment come to arise[48] and how they come to full perfection.

And further still, Brothers, the disciple lives in Contemplation of Internal Phenomena, namely, of the 'Four Holy Truths'. The disciple, Brothers, perceives according to truth ' This (i. e., The Five Khandhas) is Suffering'; perceives according to truth : ' This (i. e., Taṇhā) is the Cause of Suffering'; perceives according to truth : ' This (i. e., Nibbāna) is the Cessation of Suffering ; perceives according to truth : ' This (i. e., the Eight-fold Path) is the Path that leads to the Cessation of Suffering.'

The Four Holy Truths.

Thus he contemplates Internal Phenomena in himself; thus he contemplates Internal Phenomena in others ; thus he contemplates Internal Phenomena both in himself and in others. He perceives how Internal Phenomena arise ; perceives how Internal Phenomena pass away ; perceives the arising and the passing away of Internal Phenomena. ' Internal Phenomena only are there ' : this clear knowledge is present to him just because he possesses understanding, possesses insight, and he lives independent, unattached to anything in the world. Thus, Brothers, does the disciple dwell in Contemplation of Internal Phenomena.

---

47. " Dependent upon Eye and Forms arise Ten Fetters. Dependent upon agreeable forms, the Fetter of Sensuous-Craving arises. Dependent upon disagreeable forms the Fetter of Ill-humour arises, etc."

(Commentary.)

48. " Joy is aroused by contemplation upon the Buddha, the Truth the Holy Brotherhood, Virtue, Liberality, and so forth."

(Commentary.)

The only way, Brothers, that leads mortals to the attainment of purity, to the overcoming of sorrow and lamentation, to the cessation of suffering and grief, to the entering upon the right path, to the realisation of Nibbāna, is the ' Four Fundamentals of Attentiveness.'

Just, Brothers, as the elephant hunter drives a huge stake into the ground and chains the wild elephant to it by the neck, so as to drive out of him his wonted forest ways, so as to drive out of him his wonted forest desires, so as to drive out of him his wonted forest unruliness, obstinacy, and violence, and to accustom him to the environment of the village, and to teach him such good behaviour as is required among men ;—in like manner also, Brothers, the holy disciple has to fix his mind firmly to these ' Four Fundamentals of Attentiveness,' so that he may drive out of himself his wonted worldly ways, so that he may drive out of himself wonted worldly desires, so that he may drive out of himself his wonted worldly unruliness, obstinacy, and violence and win. to the true, and realise Nibbāna.

THE EIGHTH LINK OF THE PATH.

RIGHT CONCENTRATION, SAMMA-SAMADHI.[49]

What is Concentration ?
One-pointedness of mind (Citt'ekagattā), Brothers,—this is Samādhi or Concentration.[50]

The Objects of Concentration.
The ' Four Fundamentals of Attentiveness ' or Satipaṭṭhānas (Cf. Seventh Link), —these are the Objects of Concentration.

The Requisites for Concentration.
The ' Four Great Efforts ' (Cf. Sixth Link),—these are the means necessary for Concentration.

Bhavana.
The practicing, cultivating and developing of these things is called Bhāvanā or the Culture of Concentration.

If, Brothers, the disciple is living a holy life of virtue, is possessed of mastery over the senses and filled with clear consciousness, he seeks out a dwelling in a solitary place, in the forest, at the foot of a tree or under a rock, in a grotto, or a mountain cave; in a burial-ground or in a thicket in the woods or upon a couch of straw in the open plain.

At midday, when he has partaken of the food that he has begged, he sits himself down with legs crossed, body erect, mind present and fixed.

---

49. Sammā-samādhi in its widest sense is that concentration, which is present in every good thought (Kusala-citta). Micchā-samādhi (Wrong Concentration) is that which is present in every evil thought (Akusala-citta) and hence is only possible in the sensuous sphere not in the Trances. The Abhidhamma even speaks of a Kāmāvacara-kusala-jhāna and of a Kāmāvacara-akusala-jhāna ; that is, of absorption in good or in evil thought belonging to the sensuous sphere. Samādhi used alone, always stands for Sammā-samādhi.

50. Sammā-samādhi has two degrees of perfection, the weaker degree being called Upacāra-samādhi (Neighbourhood Concentration) and the more powerful, Appanā-samādhi (Full Concentration), which latter is the concentration that accompanies the Four Jhānas. The attainment of the Jhānas however is not a requisite for the realisation of the Four Paths and Nibbāna and neither Upacāra-samādhi nor Appanā-samādhi, as such, in any way possess the power of conferring entry into the Four Ultramundane Paths ; (See Note, 22) hence they really have no power to free one permanently from evil things The realisation of the Four Paths is only possible at the moment of deep Insight (Vipassanā) into the Transiency, Suffering, and Unsubstantiality of all Five Aspects of Existence. This Vipassanā however is attainable only during Upacāra-samādhi ; therefore, one who has entered the Jhānas must return to Upacāra-samādhi in order, through deep Vipassanā, to reach Arahatship, i. e., the entrance into Kiles-aparinibbāna, or the complete extinction of passions. (See Note, 9.)

The Arahan who has realised Nibbāna without having ever entered the Jhānas, is called Sukkhavipassaka ; literally, one whose passions, as it were, are dried up by Vipassanā. The Arahan again, who has taken Samatha, the unshakable inward tranquillity won through the Jhānas, as his vehicle (Yāna)—he is called, Samathayānaka.

He has cast away Lust; he dwells with thoughts free
from Lust; from Lust he cleanses his heart.

Absence of the Five Hindrances. He has cast away Anger; he dwells in
thoughts free from Anger, cherishing love
and compassion toward all living beings, he cleanses his
heart from Anger.

He has cast away Laxness, he dwells free from Laxness; loving the light, with watchful mind, with clear consciousness, he cleanses his mind from Laxness.

He has cast away Restless Brooding; he dwells with
mind undisturbed, with heart full of peace, he cleanses his
mind from Restless Brooding.

He has cast away Doubt; he dwells free from Doubt;
full of confidence in the good, he cleanses his heart from
Doubt.

He has put aside these 'Five Hindrances' and learnt
to know the paralysing corruptions of the mind.

1. Far from the impressions that allure the senses,
far from evil things, but still Reasoning
The Four Jhanas or Trances. and Reflecting, he enters into the First
Trance that is full of the Joy and Happiness
that is born of Concentration.

The First Trance, Brothers, is free from five things;
and there are five things present. If, Brothers, the disciple
enters into the First Trance, Lust is suppressed, Anger is
suppressed, Laxness is suppressed, Restless Brooding is
suppressed, Doubts are suppressed, and there are present,
Reasoning, Reflection,[51] Joy, Happiness, and Concentration.

2. And further, Brothers, after the suppression of Reasoning and Reflecting, whilst still retaining Joy and Happiness, the disciple, free from Reasoning and Reflecting, ob-
tains the inward peace and Oneness of mind that is born of
Concentration,—he gains the Second Trance.[52]

3. And further, Brothers; after the paling of Joy the
disciple, dwells in equanimity, with sense alert, clearly conscious, and experiences in his heart that feeling of which
holy men say: ' Happy lives the man of equanimity and
thoughtful mind,'—thus he enters the Third Trance.[53]

51. Vitakka and Vicāra (the laying hold of an abstract thought, and
continued abstract thinking) are verbal functions (Vacī-saṅkhāra).
52. The Second Trance consists of Pīti, Sukha, and Citt'ekaggatā
(Samādhi); or, Joy, Happiness, and Concentration.
53. The Third Trance consists of Sukha and Citt'ekaggatā; or, (tran-
quil) Happiness, and Concentration.

4. And further, Brothers ; when the disciple has thus rejected pleasure and pain, and has renounced previous joy and sorrow, then he enters into a state of Equanimity, free from pleasure and free from pain, into the neutral, clear-minded state of the Fourth Trance.[54]

This, Brothers, is called Right Concentration.[55]

Suppose, Brothers, that the disciple has reached the First Trance; none the less whatsoever there is of Form, of Sensation, of Perception, of Subjective Differentiations, of Consciousness,—he regards all these phenomena as Transient (Anicca), as Painful (Dukkha), as empty and void of substantiality (Anattā) and turning himself away from these things, he directs his mind towards the abiding, thus: ' This is the peace, this is the sublime goal, namely the cessation of all existence, the getting rid of every form of becoming, the annihilation of Craving (Taṇhā), the turning away from greed,—cessation and Nibbāna,' and in this state he realises Nibbāna (as Samathayānaka Arahaṁ, See Note, 50).

The Samatha-yanaka.

But even should he fail to reach Nibbāna, yet because he has desire for the truth, because he finds delight in the truth, after the annihilation of the Five Fetters (See Note, 25) that bind to the lower existence (World of the five senses, Kāma-loka), he will be objectified in a higher sphere[56] whence he returns no more (Anāgāmi) but enters Nibbāna(as Samathayānaka Anāgāmi, Cf. Note, 50).

Or suppose that he has reached the Second, or the Third, or the Fourth Trance. None the less whatsoever there is of Form, of Sensation, of Perception, of Subjective Differentiations, of Consciousness,—he regards all these phenomena as transient (Anicca), as painful (Dukkha), as

54. The Fourth Trance consists of Upekkhā and Citt'ekaggatā ; or, Equanimity and Concentration.

55. All four Jhānas or Trances may be obtained by means of ' Anāpānasati ' or, Watching over In and Out-breathing, as well as through the Meditation of Equanimity (Upekkhā-bhāvanā).
The three Sublime Meditations of Good-will (Mettā-bhāvanā), of Compassion (Karuṇā-bhāvanā), and of Sympathy (Muditā-bhāvanā), may lead to the attainment of the first three Jhānas. The ' Cemetery Meditations,' as also the Meditation upon the Impurities of the Body (Asubha-bhāvanā), can at best, only produce the first Jhāna.
The Analysis of the Body and the Contemplations upon the Buddha, the Truth, the Holy Brotherhood, Virtue, Liberality, and so forth, can only produce Upacāra-samādhi. (See Note, 50.)

56. Beings in the Sphere of Pure Form (Rūpa—loka), that is,—free from sensuality (Kāma), and beings in the Formless-Sphere (Arūpa-loka), are objectified without the instrumentality of parents.

empty and void of substantiality (Anattā), and turning himself away from these things, he directs his mind towards the abiding, thus : ' This is the peace, this is the sublime goal, namely, the cessation of all existence, the getting rid of every form of becoming, the annihilation of Craving (Taṇhā), the turning away from greed,—cessation, and Nibbāna,' and in this state he realises Nibbāna.

But even should he fail to reach Nibbāna, yet, because he has desire for the truth, because he finds delight in the truth, after the annihilation of the Five Fetters that bind to the lower existence he will be objectified in a higher sphere whence he returns no more, but enters Nibbāna.

Or again, Brothers, suppose that with heart full of Love, one penetrates, one direction, then a second, then a third, then a fourth, above and below, and round about in every quarter, and identifying himself with all, penetrates the entire world with heart of Love, grown great, wide, deep, boundless, free from wrath and anger ; or suppose that he penetrates the entire world with heart full of Compassion,— or with heart full of Joy, or with heart full of Equanimity. Whatsoever there is of Form, of Sensation, of Perception, of Subjective Differentiations, of Consciousness,—all these phenomena he regards as transient (Anicca), as Painful (Dukkha), as empty and void of substantiality (Anattā), and turning himself away from these things, he directs his mind toward the abiding, thus : ' This is the peace, this is the sublime goal, namely, the cessation of all existence, the getting rid of every form of becoming, the annihilation of Craving, the turning away from greed,—cessation and Nibbāna,' and in this state he realises Nibbāna.

The Four Sublime Meditations :
1. Metta-bhavana, or the Meditation of Love.
2. Karuna-bhavana or Meditation of Compassion.
3. Mudita-bhavana or Meditation of Sympathy.
4. Upekkha-bhavana or the Meditation of Equanimity.

But even should he fail to reach Nibbāna, yet, because he has desire for the truth, because he finds delight in the truth, after the annihilation of the Five Fetters that bind to the lower existence, he will be objectified in a higher sphere whence he returns no more, but enters Nibbāna.

4

1. But suppose, Brothers, after the complete suppression of form-perceptions,[57] after the annihilation of reflex-perceptions[58] through not reflecting upon the idea of multiplicity,[59] having the idea, 'boundless is space,' that he enters the Sphere of Boundless Space— or suppose that after the complete suppression of the Sphere of Boundless Space, having the idea, ' Boundless is Consciousness,' he enters the Sphere of Boundless Consciousness or suppose that after the complete suppression of the Sphere of Boundless Consciousness, having the idea, ' Nothing is there ' he enters the Sphere of Nothingness. Nevertheless, whatsoever there is of Sensation, of Perception, of Subjective Differentiations, of Consciousness, [60]—all these phenomena he regards as transient (Anicca), as painful (Dukkha), as empty and void of substantiality, (Anattā, and turning himself away from these things, he directs his mind towards the abiding, thus : ' This is the peace, this is the sublime goal, the cessation of all existence, the getting rid of every form of becoming, the annihilation of Craving (Taṇhā), the turning away from greed,—cessation and Nibbāna,' and in this state he realises Nibbāna.

The Four Arupayatanas or Formless Realms.

But even should he fail to reach Nibbāna, yet, because he has desire for the truth, because he finds delight in the truth, after the annihilation of the Five Fetters that bind to the lower existence, he will be objectified in a higher sphere whence he returns no more, but enter Nibbāna.

Or, Brothers, after the complete suppression of the Sphere of Nothingness, the disciple reaches the Sphere of Semi—Perception.[61]

Nirodha-Samapattl.

57. That is. after the suppression of the phenomena that belong to the Sphere of Pure Form ; as, for example, of the purely Mental Reflex (Patibhāga-Nimitta, in appearance like a glowing star, which in certain Meditations accompanies the Four Jhānas.

58. That is after the suppression of the perception of sense-objects, such as forms, sounds, odours, tastes, and bodily contacts.

59. In other words :—When the perception of sense-objects which reappear in pure Thought-Consciousness, is suppressed.

60. The Aspect of Material Existence (Rûpa) disappears upon entrance into the Arupāyatanas cr Formless Realms.

61. It is said in the Abhidhamma that the Four Arupāyatanas or Formless Realms, sometimes called Arupajjhānas, are to be understood as being supplementary to the Fourth Jhāna or Trance in the Form Sphere. (See Note, 54.) All eight states however as such are mundane (lokya) conditions and may therefore be obtained even by a Puthujjana or Worldling. They may produce *temporary* conditions of mundane happiness and may also be useful as a means of calming the mind, preparatory to practising Vipassanā, but they are powerless to produce the Four Ultramundane (lokuttar.) Paths *i.e.* to free one permanently from evil qualities. (See Note, 50.)

After the complete suppression of the sphere of Semi-perception, the disciple reaches the 'Cessation of Perception and Sensation.'[62]

Verily, Brothers, this is the highest, this is the holiest wisdom; namely, to know that all Suffering has vanished away. He has found the true deliverance that lies beyond the reach of any change.

The Goal.

This, Brothers, is verily the highest, this is the holiest truth; namely, that which is real and true: Nibbāna.

This, Brothers, is verily the highest, this is the holiest renunciation; namely, to separate one's self from all attachments.

This, Brothers, is verily the highest, this is the holiest peace; namely, to be released from Greed, Anger, and Delusion.

'I am,' Brothers, is a vain thought; 'I am not' is a vain thought; 'I shall be' is a vain thought;
The Silent Thinker. 'I shall not be' is a vain thought; 'I shall have a form' is a vain thought; 'I shall be formless' is a vain thought; 'I shall be conscious' is a vain thought; 'I shall be unconscious' is a vain thought; 'I shall be neither conscious nor unconscious' is a vain thought. To have vain thoughts, Brothers, is to be ill; to have vain thoughts is to suffer pain; if however, Brothers, all vain thoughts are overcome, one is called a 'Silent Thinker.' And the thinker, Brothers, the silent one, does not arise, does not pass away, does not die, does not tremble, does not desire. For, Brothers, there is nothing in him, that he should arise. Because he does not arise, how should he pass away? Because he does not pass away, how should he die? Because he does not die, how should he tremble? Because he does not tremble, how should he desire?

---

62. This unconscious,—as it were—cataleptic state, (in Pāli, Nirodha-samāpatti) as well as any of the Jhānas, may last for a period of fully seven days.
In the Mahāveddalla-Sutta (Majjhima-Nikāya, 43) it is said, that the state of Nirodha-Samāpatti differs from death in that it is a *temporary* and not a *total* cessation of the bodily, verbal and mental functions; death however, means in addition, the cessation of Āyu ('Vitality) and of Usmā (Heat.)
In the Abbhidhamma it is said that Nirodha-Samāpatti is only attained by a few Anāgāmis and Arahans and that it is neither mundane (lokya) since the Kāma, Rūpa and Arūpa worlds are for the time being extinguished—nor yet ultra-mundane (lokuttara) and therefore, notwithstanding that many think to the contrary, it is in no way identical with Nibbāna. (See Note, 13.)

Hence, Brothers, the reward of asceticism is neither alms, nor honour, nor fame, nor the virtues that appertain to the Order, nor the rap-

The True Goal.

ture of concentration, nor clear wisdom. That Unshakable Deliverance of the Mind, however, Brothers,—that verily is the object, that is Arahatship, that is the heart of asceticism, that is its Goal.

And those, Brothers, who formerly in the past were Blessed Ones, Perfectly Enlightened Ones (Buddhas).— These also have pointed out to their disciples the self-same goal as has been pointed out by me to my disciples. And those, Brothers, who afterwards, in the future shall become Blessed Ones, Perfectly Enlightened Ones—these Blessed Ones also shall point out to their disciples the self-same goal as has been pointed out by me to my disciples.

Verily, Brothers, whatsoever a master owes to his dis-

The Great Command.

ciples, impelled by love and sympathy, moved by compassion,—that have you received from me. Here, trees invite; there, lonely solitudes. Devote yourselves to contemplation, Bro-thers, that sloth may not come over you, that later you may not have to repent you. Hold this as our command!

All life is transient. By diligence attain your Goal!

APPENDIX.

DISCOURSE ON THE GREAT FORTY-FOLD TRAIN OF IDEAS.

Thus have I heard. The Blessed One once dwelt in the Jeta-wood near Sāvatthī, at Anāthapiṇḍika's hermitage. There the Blessed One addressed the mendicant monks. "Brothers," he said. "Lord!" replied those monks to the Blessed One. And the Blessed One said: "Holy and Right Concentration,[1] Brothers, let me point out to you, with its necessary endowments, with its accompaniments. Wherefore hearken and give good heed to my words." "Yea Lord!" replied those monks to the Blessed One. And the Blessed One said.

"But what, Brothers, is Holy and Right Concentration, with its necessary endowments, with its accompaniments? One-pointedness of mind, Brothers, which is accompanied by seven things, namely,—by Right Understanding, Right Mindedness, Right Speech, Right Action, Right Living, Right Effort, Right Attentiveness,—this, Brothers, is called Holy and Right Concentration with its necessary endowments, with its accompaniments.

Now, Right Understanding, Brothers, takes the first place. But how, Brothers does Right Understanding take the first place? When one knows evil views as evil views and right understanding as right understanding, then one has Right Understanding. But what, Brothers, are evil views? 'Alms, gifts, and the making of offerings are all useless. There is no fruit, no result, either of good or of evil actions. There are no such things as this life and the next life. Father and mother, as also purely spiritual beings, are mere words. There are no ascetics and holy men in the world who are spotless and perfect, who can explain

---

1. That is,—the concentration (for the two degree of concentration, See Note 50), which is possessed by the Holy Disciples (Ariya-sāvaka), i.e. those that have attained to one or the other of the Four Ultramundane (lokuttara) Paths, the Sotāpanna, the Sakadāgāmi, the Anāgāmi, the Arahaṁ.

The Eightfold Path which they practise is called the Holy Eightfold Path to distinguish it from the Eightfold Path of the Puthujjana or Worldling.

this life and the next life which they themselves have perceived.' These, Brothers, are evil views.

But what, Brothers, is Right Understanding ? Right Understanding, Brothers, let me tell you, is of two kinds. There is, Brothers, a Right Understanding which is of the world, yields worldly fruits and brings good results ; and there is, Brothers, a Holy and Right Understanding which not of the world but is ultramundane (lokuttara) and conjoined with the Path.

But what, Brothers, is Right Understanding which is of the world, yields worldly fruits and brings good results ? 'Alms, gifts and the making of offerings are useful. There is fruit, there is result, both of good and of evil actions. There are such things as this life and the next life. Father and mother, as also purely spiritual beings, are not mere words. There are in the world ascetics and holy men who are spotless and perfect, who can explain this life and the next life, which they themselves have perceived.' This Brothers, is Right Understanding which is of the world, yields worldly fruits, and brings good results.

But what, Brothers, is Holy and Right Understanding which is not of the world, but is ultramundane and conjoined with the Path ?

Whatsoever there is of wisdom, of the faculty of wisdom, of the power of wisdom, of penetration, of right understanding, conjoined with the Path,—the mind being holy, being turned away from the world and conjoined with the Path, the holy Path being pursued,—this, Brothers, is called Holy and Right Understanding, which is not of the world, but is ultramundane and conjoined with the Path. Now, in making efforts to overcome evil views, to arouse Right Understanding, one practises Right Effort, and in overcoming evil views with attentive mind and dwelling with attentive mind in possession of Right Understanding, one practises Right Attentiveness. Hence there are three things that accompany and follow upon Right Understanding, namely,—Right Understanding, Right Effort, and Right Attentiveness.

Now, Right Understanding, Brothers, takes the first place. But how, Brothers does right understanding take the first place ? When one knows evil mindedness as evil mindedness and Right Mindedness as Right Mindedness,— then one has Right Understanding. But what, Brothers, is evil mindedness. Sensuous thoughts, malevolent thoughts, cruel thoughts,—this, Brothers, is called evil mindedness.

But what, Brothers, is Right Mindedness ? Right Minded-ness, Brothers, let me tell you, is of two kinds.   There is, Brothers, a Right Mindedness which is of the world, yields worldly fruits and brings good results, and there is, Brothers, a Right Mindedness which is not of the world but is ultra-mundane and conjoined with the Path.

But what, Brothers, is Right Mindedness which is of the world, yields worldly fruits and brings good results ? The thought of renouncing worldly ways ; the thought of bearing no ill will ; the thought of abstaining from cruelty, —this, Brothers, is Right Mindedness which is of the world, yields worldly fruits and brings good results.

But what, Brothers, is Holy and Right Mindedness which is not of the world but is ultramundane and conjoined with the Path ?   Whatsoever there is of thinking, consider-ing, reasoning, thought, ratiocination, application,—the mind being holy, being turned away from the world and con-joined with the Path, the holy Path being pursued,—these verbal operations of the mind, Brothers, are called Holy and Right Mindedness, which is not of the world, but is ultra-mundane and conjoined with the Path.   Now in making efforts to overcome evil mindedness, to arouse Right Minded-ness, one practises Right Effort, and in overcoming evil mindedness with attentive mind and dwelling with attentive mind in possession of Right Mindedness, one practises Right Attentiveness. Hence there are three things that accompany and follow upon Right Mindedness, namely,—Right Under-standing, Right Effort, and Right Attentiveness.

Now, Right Understanding, Brothers, takes the first place.   But how, Brothers does Right Understanding take the first place ? When one knows evil speech as evil speech and Right Speech as Right Speech,—then one has right Understanding.   But what, Brothers, is evil speech ? Lying, slandering, using harsh language, vain talk,—this, Brothers, is evil speech.

But what, Brothers, is Right Speech ? Right speech, Brothers, let me tell you, is of two kinds.   There is, Brothers, a Right Speech which is of the world, yields worldly fruits and brings good results and there is, Brothers, a Holy and Right Speech which is not of the world but is ultramundane and conjoined with the Path.

But what, Brothers, is Right Speech which is of the world, yields worldly fruits and brings good results ? Abstain-ing from Lying, abstaining from Slandering, abstaining from Harsh Language, abstaining from Vain Talk,—this, Brothers, is Right Speech which is of the world, yields wordly fruits and brings good results.

But what, Brothers, is Holy and Right Speech which is not of the world, but is ultramundane and conjoined with the Path? The abhorrence of the practice of the four-fold evil speech, the abstaining, withholding, refraining therefrom, the mind being holy, being turned away from the world and conjoined with the Path, the holy Path being pursued, —this, Brothers, is called Holy and Right speech, which is not of the world, but is ultramundane and conjoined with the Path. Now in making efforts to overcome evil speech, to arouse Right Speech, one practises Right Effort, and in overcoming evil speech with attentive mind and dwelling with attentive mind in possession of Right Speech, one practises Right Attentiveness. Hence there are three things that accompany and follow upon Right Speech, namely,—Right Understanding, Right Effort, and Right Attentiveness.

Now, Right Understanding, Brothers, takes the first place. But how, Brothers does Right Understanding take the first place? When one knows evil action as evil action and Right Action as Right Action,—then one has Right Understanding. But what, Brothers, is evil action? Killing, Stealing, Indulging in unlawful Sexual Intercourse,—this, Brothers, is evil action.

But what, Brothers, is Right Action? Right Action, Brothers, let me tell you, is of two kinds. There is, Brothers, a Right Action which is of the world, yields worldly fruits and brings good results; and there is, Brothers, a Holy and Right Action which is not of the world but is ultramundane and conjoined with the Path.

But what, Brothers, is Right Action which is of the world, yields worldly fruits and brings good results? Abstaining from Killing, abstaining from Stealing, abstaining from Indulgence in Unlawful Sexual Intercourse—this, Brothers, is Right Action which is of the world, yields worldly fruits and brings good results.

But what, Brothers, is Holy and Right Action which is not of the world, but is ultramundane and conjoined with the Path? The abhorrence of the practice of the three-fold evil action the abstaining, withholding, refraining therefrom, the mind being holy, being turned away from the world and conjoined with the Path, the holy Path being pursued,—this, Brothers, is called Holy and Right Action, which is not of the world, but is ultramundane and conjoined with the Path. Now, in making efforts to overcome evil action, to arouse Right Action, one practises Right Effort, and in overcoming evil action with attentive mind and dwelling with attentive mind in possession of Right Action, one practises Right Attentiveness. Hence there are three things that accompany and follow upon Right Action, namely,—Right Understanding, Right Effort, and Right Attentiveness.

Now, Right Understanding, Brothers, takes the first place. But how, Brothers, does Right Understanding take the first place? When one knows evil living as evil living and Right Living as Right Living,—then one has Right Understanding. But what, Brothers, is evil living? To practise deceit, treachery, soothsaying, trickery, usury,—this, Brothers, is evil living.

But what, Brothers, is Right Living? Right Living, Brothers, let me tell you, is of two kinds. There is, Brothers, a Right Living which is of the world, yields worldly fruits and brings good results and there is, Brothers, a Holy and Righ· Living which is not of the world but is ultramundane and conjoined with the Path.

But what, Brothers, is Right Living which is of the world, yields worldly fruits and brings good results? When the noble disciple, having given up evil living, gets his livelihood by a right way of living,—this, Brothers, is Right Living which is of the world, yields worldly fruits and brings good results.

But what, Brothers, is Holy and Right Living, which is not of the world, but is ultramundane and conjoined with the Path? The abhorrence of evil living, the abstaining, withholding, refraining therefrom,—the mind being holy, being turned away from the world and conjoined with the Path, the holy Path being pursued,—this, Brothers, is called Holy and Right Living, which is not of the world, but is ultramundane and conjoined with the Path. Now in making efforts to overcome evil living, to arouse Right Living, one practises Right Effort, and in overcoming evil living with attentive mind and dwelling with attentive mind in possession of Right Living, one practises Right Attentiveness. Hence there are three things that accompany and follow upon Right Living. namely,—Right Understanding, Right Effort, and Right Attentiveness.

Now, Right Understanding Brothers takes the first place. But how, Brothers, does Right Understanding take the first place? Whoso, Brothers, has Right Understanding, has Right Mindedness. Whoso has Right Mindedness, has Right Speech. Whoso has Right Speech, has

Right Action. Whoso has Right Action, has Right Living. Whoso has Right Living, has Right Effort. Whoso has Right Effort, has Right Attentiveness. Whoso has Right Attentiveness, has Right Concentration. Whoso has Right Concentration has Right Knowledge. Whoso has Right Knowledge, has found the true Deliverance.

. Thus, Brothers, the eight-fold equipped Striver for Holiness (Sekho) realises the Ten Constituents of Arahatship.

Now, Right Understanding, Brothers, takes the first place. But how, Brothers, does Right Understanding take the first place? For him, Brothers, who is possessed of Right Understanding, evil views have ceased, and the various evil, unwholesome things which may arise through evil views,—these also have ceased; and through Right Understanding the various wholesome things attain to full perfection. For him, Brothers, who is possessed of Right Mindedness, possessed of Right Speech, of Right Action, Right Living, Right Effort, Right Attentiveness, Right Concentration, Right Knowledge, and true Deliverance,— evil mindedness has ceased, evil speech has ceased, evil action has ceased, evil living, evil effort, evil attentiveness, evil concentration, evil knowledge, and false deliverance, have ceased; and the various evil and unwholesome things which may arise through false deliverance,—these also have ceased; and through True Deliverance the various wholesome things attain to full perfection.

Thus, Brothers, is set before your a Great Forty-fold Train of Ideas, with twenty wholesome parts, with twenty unwholesome parts, and none can gainsay it,—neither ascetics nor priests, nor invisible beings, nor God nor Devil, nor anyone whatsoever in all the wrolds. For, whosoever, Brothers, of ascetics or priests should deem it fitting to disparage, to vilify this Great Forty-fold Train of Ideas, the reproaches of such an one concerning these ten points, even in this present life would turn to his own reproach. For, if such an one disparages Right Understanding, then he honours and exalts those ascetics and priests of evil views; if he disparages Right Mindedness, Right Speech, Right Action, Right Living, Right Effort, Right Attentiveness, Right Concentration, Right Knowledge, and True Deliverance,—then he honours and exalts those ascetics and priests of Evil Mindedness, Evil Speech, Evil Action, Evil Living, Evil Effort, Evil Attentiveness, Evil Concentration, Evil Knowledge, and False Deliverance. For whosoever, Brothers, of ascetics or priests should deem it fitting to disparage, to vilify this Great Forty-fold Train of

Ideas, the reproaches of such an one concerning these ten points, even in this present life would turn to his own reproach.

Even, Brothers, the teachers of fatalism or those who deny the result of action, or those who believe nothing—even these do not deem it fitting to disparage, to vilify this Great Forty-fold Train of Ideas. And why ? Even through fear of incurring blame ; through fear of arousing opposition and annoyance.

Thus spake the Blessed One ; and pleased and delighted, those monks applauded the words of the Blessed One.

Sutta No. 17, Majjhima Nikāya.

Printed in the USA
CPSIA information can be obtained
at www.ICGtesting.com
LVHW010421300923
759528LV00010B/1210